THE ACTION GAP

BUSINESS STRATEGIES FOR CO-PROSPERITY

New World thinking
for conscious leaders
and managers

DILLPREIT KAUR

PARTRIDGE

Library of Congress Control Number:		2024902805
ISBN:	Hardcover	978-1-5437-8127-4
	Softcover	978-1-5437-8126-7
	eBook	978-1-5437-8128-1

To order additional copies of this book, contact
Toll Free +65 3165 7531 (Singapore)
Toll Free +60 3 3099 4412 (Malaysia)
orders.singapore@partridgepublishing.com

www.partridgepublishing.com/singapore

An Ode

When we give our own power away,
maybe sometime in the past and we forgot about it
or in more recent times,
we experience an imbalance state,
a quiet disharmony within ourselves.

For some, this state manifests gradually.
For others, it is almost dormant until something happens,
while for the rest of us, it is a daily feeling of resentment,
anger, unfairness, and we cope with complaints and rants.

What is dangerous is that, in this state,
we may not know that we might also be taking another's power away,
creating further imbalance.

We can break this cycle.
It starts with dignity consciousness.

We are all born with equal self-worth.
Social constructs, judgements, and expectations
made us feel otherwise.

This book is therefore a call for us, especially leaders,
to recognise we are all worthy.

CONTENTS

▲

ACKNOWLEDGEMENTS

For experiences shared in this book, I am much indebted to stakeholders I worked with from around the world. Thank you for trusting me with your ideas, visions and hopes for stronger and more inclusive institutions. For invaluable help along the way, I thank Braema Mathi, Dr Wilhelm Hofmeister, Christian Echle, Jia Rong Low, Paul Singh Gill, Esther An, Melissa Ho and Jasvir Kaur.

INTRODUCTION

Weaving is a common tradition in many of our ethnic communities in Asia especially. This book is many years in the making, intricately weaving my knowledge and insights journey within the systems of sustainability development, spanning more than a decade. It involves my experiences from studying in Singapore, Pretoria, Sydney, and Kathmandu as well as working with Asia Pacific and European change makers. I have worked in what may seem like random fields: human rights, political party building, Internet governance, technology start-up venture building, and most recently, corporate sustainability, unknowingly knowing everything is interconnected.

This book hopes to seed the new future with a vision of what it could be with practical steps. I hope it is a resource to many about sustainable self-leadership and organisational growth (whatever that might look like for you). Also, there is a procedural essence to building something of quality over time. If we are talking about societal impact or breaking intergenerational cycles of poverty, addiction, powerlessness, then even more so we need to create building models that have a clear vision of a desirable outcome and tangible, simple and teachable steps towards breaking out of one. This book hopes to help co-create that model with you.

Unpacking Sustainable Development

There are several discourses when it comes to sustainability that are well analysed in *Green Utopias: Environmental Hope Before and After Nature* by Lisa Garforth. Specifically, Lisa makes a differentiation between the aims of two well-known reports that have come to shape how we perceive sustainability today. The first, 1972 'The Limits to Growth' (LTG) report recognised that because of inequalities of economic wealth and industrial development between countries, growth will eventually need to stop for People and the planet,[1] while the later 1987 Brundtland Report premises that 'it is development itself that is to be made sustainable.'[2]

For the LTG report, finite natural resources was the cause for environmental crisis, while for the Brundtland report, it is how we grow that is the cause. This is because in 1972, the LTG report used a singular, absolute, and physical worldview while Brundtland adopted a multiple, staggered, and social one.[3] Lisa posits these differences in root causes of environmental problems do not matter because we need to accelerate pathways towards sustainability now.[4]

'Since the policy framework on climate change that emerged in the United Nations Framework Convention on Climate Change (UNFCCC) in 1992, the next fifteen years saw a solidification of scientific consensus that climate change is real, anthropogenic, and consequential'.[5] It was in 1992 with Agenda 21 that marked the moment at which sustainable development became a goal for policymakers. By the 1990s, corporate sustainability responsibility and shareholder engagement came to the fore for companies as well.

The mid-2000s, after the fourth Intergovernmental Panel on Climate Change (IPCC) report and Stern review, saw a period of consensus on climate change and optimism with popular media and consumers alike.[6] It was in 2005, when Environment, Social, and Governance (ESG) was coined by the United Nations (UN) Global Compact, which was later embedded in the UN Principles for Responsible Investment in 2006. More hope with the Bali Road map in 2007.

---

[1]   L. Garforth, *Green Utopias: Environmental Hope Before and After Nature*, Cambridge, John Wiley and Sons, 2017, pp. 83-6; 90-100, **[e-book].**

[2]   Garforth, *Green Utopias*, p.119.

[3]   Garforth, *Green Utopias*, pp. 119-20.

[4]   Garforth, *Green Utopias*, pp. 72-4.

[5]   Garforth, *Green Utopias*, p. 269.

[6]   Garforth, *Green Utopias*, pp. 275-76.

By 2015, the UN Sustainable Development Goals (SDGs) with its 169 indicators and 17 goals were etched, building from its predecessor framework—the Millennium Development Goals (MDGs) from 2000 to 2015. As 2030 draws close, which is the milestone year for achieving the SDGs, it is unlikely all goals will be met given the four-trillion-dollar financial gap for developing economies in sustainable development investments.[7] Moreover, we have raised our climate ambition to reach net zero by 2050 earliest for most economies, according to publicly-announced sectoral and country road maps, with some exceptions prior to and some after 2050.

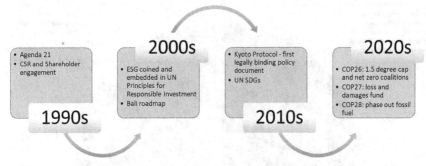

Figure 1: Summary of global climate policy high-level developments

Moving forward though, we need to avoid the 'performance or management of unsustainability' as proposed by Ingolfur Bluhdorn.[8] In *Green Utopias*, Garforth urges us to think about how we live in uncertainty and emerging environmental risks while making the shifts to more ethical alternatives to mitigate these very risks.[9] While 'deep ecology holds that new forms of ecological consciousness and environmental ethics grows best in communities that are small, self-sufficient, stable and autonomous', most of our cities are not built this way. As such, an eco-centric world would be a call for 'renewal and emancipation' and 'collective politics' where we start seeing nature and culture, the material and the social, the objective and subjective as a sum of a whole and not separate.[10] We all have a part to play.

---

[7]   UN News, *Developing countries face $4 trillion investment gap in SDGs*, 5 July 2023, https://news.un.org/en/story/2023/07/1138352 (accessed 26 January 2024).
[8]   Garforth, *Green Utopias*, p. 306, **[e-book]**.
[9]   Garforth, *Green Utopias*, p. 309.
[10] Garforth, *Green Utopias*, p. 422.

Business Case For Sustainability

As we transit to industry 4.0, which is mainly the digital transformation of our industries and way of lives, the onus on businesses to comply and ensure economic, governance, social, ethical and environmental (EGSEE) performance has also risen.[11] Figure 2 shows these expectations from key actors in the sustainability management ecosystem and the resultant interdependent relationships that will be required to sustain and grow this nexus.

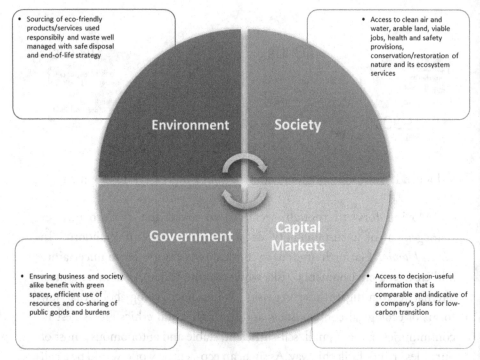

Figure 2: Business Value Creation 4.0 requires
upstream and downstream impact consideration
across different actors to accelerate change

---

11   Z. Rezaee, J. Tsui P. Cheng and G. Zhou, *Business Sustainability in Asia: Compliance, Performance, and Integrated Reporting and Assurance*, London, John Wiley and Sons, 2019, pp.6-10.

Such is systems change: it is an open space of adjacent possibilities that we can all tap into to co-create the best outcomes for our communities involved. Businesses cannot only be about people running the organisations. It has to be about a bigger vision, one that preferably aims at improving socio-economic outcomes for all and not just for a handful.

With regards to decarbonisation as it is a pertinent step towards respecting Mother Earth's finite resources for now, unless we use them in a regenerative and responsible manner, we indeed need to simplify our operations and diversify our sourcing to look for alternatives. There is more noise in the industry about the challenges than there are implementable solutions. This need not be our mindset when faced with challenges.

The sustainability solution is simple—where are we making most of our resources procured (purchased or free) and how are we best utilising it to move towards a regenerative business model that is self-sustaining with revenue reinvested in the organisation's mission or sustainable financing instruments leveraged in order to fuel more innovation and growth that is sustaining EGSEE goals?

The resource efficiency issue—what to cut back on and what is needed is where we need to begin. A lot of times we do not know who is doing what, and when asked, the staff or business partner may get defensive. We also do not track the impact variables of the products or services we provide, thinking it should work out according to what we have thought. The theory of change behind why we implement many initiatives is missing in most organisations, especially those missing a North Star. This is dangerous as it leads to reckless use of resources and often ends up as a waste of time. But even then, we do not see the folly of our ways, because of our egos or pursuit of simplistic endeavours in fear that if we critically apply ourselves, we might find the can of worms underneath the surface, probing us to really solve the situation.

The business case for sustainability emerges when we realise there are cost savings from implementing this sound rationale of thinking through why we do what we do. By ensuring we think more about the how behind what we do, we not only save money, time, and resources but start to be more compelled towards our North Stars and do better.

Sustainability is therefore as much about the individual as it is society. It is culture as much as governance. And it is meeting objectives with results that support desirable socio-economic outcomes for others. The more value we can capture with our new business models from the start, the better. And closing the loop with mindful consumption and innovative solutions to reduce waste by upcycling or reintroducing into the production cycles of our organisations will be the necessary lever for enabling the low-carbon transition. According to the World Economic Forum, circular economy models can help accelerate this momentum to net-zero energy emissions and multi-sector resource optimisation.[12]

With regards to scope 1, 2, and 3 or direct and indirect greenhouse gas emissions (GHG) reductions, a simplified model where each organisation maps out its entire value chain both upstream and downstream to make a conscious decision on how to reach carbon neutrality before reaching net zero will be foundational. By understanding what we can directly control and what we cannot, broken down into further sub-categories with regards to suppliers, for example, we can better understand where we can get started. The end goal is simple: to reduce as much as possible energy or emissions we release through our business operations. To optimise the resources, we have to make more value out of it than before, to transition towards circular economic business models.

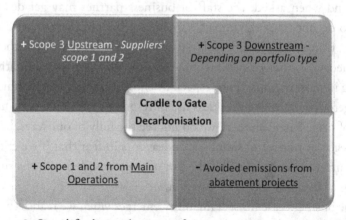

Figure 3: Simplified visualisation of emissions coverage across value chain from source (i.e. cradle) to sale of product/service (i.e. gate)

---

12   J. Long, '7 surprising facts to know about the circular economy for COP26', *World Economic Forum*, 2021, 27 October 2021, https://www.weforum.org/agenda/2021/10/7-surprising-facts-to-know-about-the-circular-economy-for-cop26/ (accessed 26 January 2024).

This will require identifying new business partners who offer low-carbon alternatives and striking partnerships within the industry to decrease the price premium through either bulk purchase via a consortium of industry leaders or association. Much like the example of sustainable aviation fuel credits mentioned above to finance the ecosystem, ingenious finance instruments will be required. And brokering new sustainable or transition finance tools with financiers including insurers and reinsurers will be helpful. The emerging risks to get to net zero are fairly unknown as near-term and long-term timelines vary across geographies. Even though there is a lag in climate change eventually manifesting, near term poses higher transition risks if climate regulations get more stringent along with stranding asset risks from more extreme weather patterns.

Such scenarios will require even more efficient resource management planning and implementation, which many firms have yet to do, understandably so as we transit out of the challenges of a public health emergency caused by COVID-19. As we understand how interconnected most things are in the world, we birth a new approach and mindset to disruption. With climate change potentially raising the likelihood of epidemics due to displacement of wildlife and/or spread of air or waterborne diseases stemming from natural disasters, the need to apply a holistic and systematic lens will grow increasingly important in the coming decades.

If anything, this should excite us as often this is where inventive solutions and innovative technology emerge. And it will only be possible if we are each empowered and enabled to realise our own creative potential to contribute to the interconnected nature of sustainability issues.

Taking Action

The meta-aim of this book is to boost understanding and engagement of different and even untraditional stakeholders when it comes to tackling sustainability challenges. We cannot do it alone. In fact, most of a company's non-financial data required for corporate reporting is compiled from stakeholders across all business units, portfolio (i.e. subsidiaries), and supply chain. According to CDP, 70–80 per cent of a company's scope 3 reporting is in their supply chains. As we know, fifteen categories of scope

3 are further streamlined to the few categories that represent at least two thirds of a company's scope 3 emissions. Based off this, further data is extrapolated. Should tenants' emissions be significant, energy, water, waste data are required from tenants listed in a company's boundary reporting, depending on whether that is equity or operational control.

However, often the virtuous effects of network and information sharing end up being hoarded by similar/elite players, further propelling inequities of power and information asymmetries, or simply not ventured because of lack of know-how or time. This leads to weak data quality, inaccuracies from human errors, and sometimes no data when many data-management solutions are in the marketplace for our picking even on a subscription basis. What is truly at the helm of the issue is the adequate knowledge and purpose for many workers with regards to why this data is required so that it is reported in a timely manner or at least uploaded to a data analytics platform accurately. With various reasons for resource constraints, communicating the outcomes can be missed out.

As such, in this book we are looking at sustainability from a bigger angle. When we can see how everything is interconnected, perhaps we may understand how our actions, no matter how big or small, play a part in the gradual transformation of systems we live, work, and play in, starting from the individual level, with one mindset and mental model at a time. This book is also about realising that our present actions come from our own past and we have power to positively change the future. As organisations are made of different individuals coming together, the transformative power of many self-aware leaders is scalable and much needed now as we grapple with many transitions and possible confusion. With each advancement we pursue, we are seeing dualistic impacts that on one hand would accelerate growth while exacerbating the socio-economic gaps either between the haves and have-nots or developed and emerging markets.

As the global pandemic of 2020 showed, we are more interconnected than ever and one lockdown or disruption in supply chain can affect us all. While increased focus on national security might help in this regard, there is more potential for us to pursue interdependence with one another. Mother Earth is abundant, and by acting responsibly, we can secure life on this planet for many more generations to come.

This book is therefore written on a premise that we each can do our part to collaborate, participate, foster, and scale social innovations needed to solve wicked problems of our brittle, anxious, non-linear, and incomprehensible (BANI) world. With great governance, leadership and management, we can contribute effective funding of much-needed social outcomes.

What are these social issues are known to us all, and many are shared problems across economies to varying scales. There is no one-size-fits-all solution as each market is culturally unique. Nevertheless, many national road maps towards sustainable development articulate an ideal vision of a fair and equitable society.

With more focus, grounded action, and blended finance with risk guarantees, we can start scaling the best practices and implementing new solutions that are emerging from our own consciousness. The need for non-financial data harvesting will grow to support both the work that businesses do to offer services and how these outcomes can align better with the real needs of consumers on the ground, to ensure business continuity is sustainable, has community buy-in, and contributes to a greater good (if that is the intent).

Figure 4: Debt financing sustainability projects in emerging markets requires risk guarantees for blended finance to work

Interdependence is here to stay, and it starts with understanding where our dependencies are within a system. Once we fix our dependencies with focused solutions, we can engage another from a place of reciprocity. We will not simply be taking or giving but equitably sharing. So much of our society is still built on inequitable sharing—from philanthropy to corporate social responsibility to welfare states because the root cause seems too difficult to tackle. As sharing economy business models show, there is increased value in leveraging on one another's strengths instead of building a bigger business case. With more resources, we can do more as well. Let this be the thinking when reading this book.

How Nature Organises Chaos

It would be a fallacy to think nature organises. I believe it is organic and accepting of all types of relationships, resulting in symbiosis most times and, sometimes, new variants of species, increasing its own richness of diversity. And this is incredible, this co-creative energy that brings forth new or better life forms and ways of being just by being as it is—accepting, receiving.

Nature teaches us easy lessons in coexistence with its many examples of symbiotic relationships, available to us at any point of time. These relationships are mutually beneficial in a non-conditional or transactional manner. The value that one gives to the other is not quantifiable but qualitatively enhances the well-being of the organism. In cases where it does not, death occurs for new life to be born again. This cycle is regenerative.

Like in the process of mycorrhizae, the symbiotic association of fungi and a plant's root system plays an important role in the uptake of essential nutrients from the soil for the plant to thrive. This is not quantifiable in terms of amount of transaction, but the coexistence enhances the lifespan of the plant, which would otherwise not last as long. Status quo can persist, but coexistence ensures a longer-term survivability especially in our increasingly volatile world with potential new pandemics, climate crises, or political upheavals.

Should we humans operate with as much acceptance and zero judgement, perhaps we may emulate these co-benefits in our societies too. And we see it in the form of carbon credits that are supporting both environmental and societal gains in terms of preserving local biodiversity and creating jobs for otherwise underserved markets. Although there is still much global discussion around the integrity of this market mechanism as well as how to incentivise corporations to reduce first before buying offsets, it is a model of co-prosperity worth scaling once it is well regulated.

For nature, chaos usually comes in the form of human-made errors such as deforestation, overfishing, over-extraction, pollution, neglecting or avoiding indigenous wisdom. Nature then 'organises' by responding to balance out its effects. Issues come when we expect nature to 'organise' linearly: Where there are droughts, we expect rain. Where there are floods, we expect, well, less rain.

With our simple model thinking, we forget we live in a highly spiritual universe with its own laws and ways of being that we need to respect. Things will not always go our way, and we live in a living ecosystem. With every action, there is a reaction. What exactly have we been putting out there and what are we truly expecting back if not a greenhouse effect? As such, the latest climate science by the Intergovernmental Panel on Climate Change (IPCC) should not be surprising given how fast so many of our economies have grown and lifestyles have changed just from the 1990s till now. In a span of three decades, we moved from floppy disks to CDs to thumb drives to bigger storage drives to the cloud! Similarly for our smartphones, smart TVs, smart living appliances. All these require energy to design, build, transport, sell, buy, throw. The whole life cycle of any product has grown exponentially with the use of more lithium batteries, for instance, which we are still figuring out how to optimise when discarded.

With bigger individual carbon footprints, continued widening of income inequalities and their related carbon footprints and struggling efforts by governments to play catch-up in regulating these actors, we humans are the sole chaos factor in the natural world. By acknowledging this fact, we can start making amends. Nature is the very basis and the end of our existence. We need fresh air, water, fertile land, and its related ecosystem services to receive the much-needed resources we need to subsist, work, live, and play. We can unlearn and re-learn how to be with nature more sustainably, and it is my personal plea that we all do so.

All Is Chaos:
Release Expectations, Set Clear Intentions

I sit at the Grote Markt in Antwerp and people-watch from a restaurant. Slightly disappointed by the *Manneken Pis*, I sit to take in the sights of the old quarter instead. It has just rained and so the market square with its cobbled pavements is wet. Not too many people are out. Dreary skies but there is a freshness in the autumn air. Unknown to me, there will be a terrorist attack in Paris tomorrow, and this city will be under lockdown. I would have narrowly made my way out towards London.

We are living in precarious times.

Chaos theory emerged in the twentieth century as a new field of scientific inquiry. The ancient Greeks seem to have accepted that order came from disorder.[13] This is a fascinating field as it reminds us that predictability is both rare and constrained by what society, governments, and norms have filtered out from the rich variance of possibilities within a rather complicated universe.[14] As such, this limits our abilities to comprehend and forecast all scenarios of complexity.[15]

Mathematician Ian Stewart defines chaos as 'the ability of simple models without inbuilt random features to generate highly irregular behaviour'.[16] Depending on the type of systems we operate in (deterministic, linear, or non-linear), a feedback loop via output affecting the inputs of a system can affect its operations. However, feedback is often ignored to create simplistic models. 'Simple relationships, even deterministic ones, appear to generate indeterminate behaviour because of varying response rates between individuals

---

[13] S. Ziauddin and A. Iwona, *Introducing Chaos: A Graphic Guide*, London, Icon Books, 2004, p.11, **[e-book]**.

[14] Ziauddin and Iwona, *Introducing Chaos*, p. 15.

[15] Ziauddin and Iwona, *Introducing Chaos*, p. 15.

[16] I. Stewart, 'Portraits of chaos: The latest ideas in geometry are combining with high-tech computer graphics – the results are providing stunning new insights into chaotic motion', *New Scientist*, 4 November 1989, https://www.newscientist.com/article/mg12416893-100-portraits-of-chaos-the-latest-ideas-in-geometry-are-combining-with-high-tech-computer-graphics-the-results-are-providing-stunning-new-insights-into-chaotic-motion/ (accessed 29 January 2024).

and organisations.'[17] We need it simple so that more people can understand at the expense of assumptions that may not be valid in times of crisis.

People do not simply react to their environment; they process their experiences and use that information to (re)create world views that result in new and different relationships. Thus, human systems differ from other systems in a fundamental way. Social domains or 'areas of social life that are organised by reference to a series of interlocking practices and values' incorporate contradictions, conflict, and negotiation within the interactions, and thereby provide an alternate and potentially richer paradigm for analysis.[18]

In line with simple models, the Madman theory, which looks at leaders who prefer following their gut over data, are unpredictable, and often ignore good advice in decision-making, has emerged.[19] This leadership style makes spontaneous decisions without consulting a process or at least a strategy alone. There is little consideration for work done before, and with a lack of other authority figures, this leader takes an all-or-nothing approach, which often leaves well-meaning experts out of the discussion. In the context of complex and emerging risks affecting businesses, such a leadership style is a risk in itself. There is an increased need now to think global as interconnected risks like the global pandemic can easily disrupt businesses of all sizes and jurisdictions. Working together and seeing the big picture while ensuring progression is key.

As such, how we perceive and react to chaos matters today especially since we are dealing with madman leaders sometimes and our models are too simplistic. Accepting that all is chaos is an important start. It leaves out surprise or disappointment when it happens as we well understand it is part of life. Understanding chaos can provide us with insights if there is an underlying way to control a system that seemed chaotic in the first place.

---

[17] ScienceDirect Topics, *Chaos Theory - an overview - Discussion 5.6*, 2024, https://www.sciencedirect.com/topics/earth-and-planetary-sciences/chaos-theory (Accessed 5 February 2024) from book - D. Etkin, *Disaster Theory: An Interdisciplinary Approach to Concepts and Causes*, Oxford, Butterworth-Heinemann, 2016.

[18] ScienceDirect Topics, *Chaos Theory - an overview - Discussion 5.6*, 2024, https://www.sciencedirect.com/topics/earth-and-planetary-sciences/chaos-theory (Accessed 5 February 2024).

[19] J. Sciutto, *The Madman Theory: Trump Takes on the World*, New York, Harper, 2020, p.13 and 205, **[e-book]**.

Sense-making will be a key practice for any leader going forward. We are inundated with much doom and gloom about inflation rates skyrocketing, cost-of-living challenges, climate-change-related extreme-weather patterns, wars creating humanitarian turmoil, terrorism threatening national security. Coupled with the various transits our societies are making towards low-carbon, greener, safer, more inclusive and smart futures (take your pick), the peak of the mountain is not in sight, and we are noticing how unfit we are and maybe we should stop, chill at a beach instead, and wait for someone else to scale the mountain first. Many would call this short-term thinking unless there is a goal to attempt the change, with more preparations and resources.

This sense-making will continue to evolve as we move into more complex inter-relational situations with the gig economy, contracting and outsourcing to cheaper labour markets, and more. Homing in on the norm of interdependence and what it means for each one of us will only support us going forward.

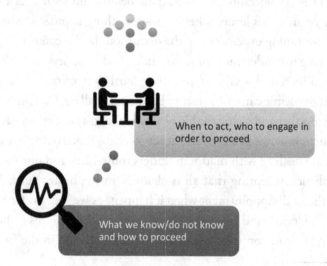

When to act, who to engage in order to proceed

What we know/do not know and how to proceed

Figure 5: Sense-making with information and relationships

Most governments are galvanising behind this change impetus fuelled by media houses and groundswell of public opinion to regulate better. These are not easy times for policymakers and regulators or for businesses. Collective effort would be required from both ends—regulators to understand business operations and business to work with regulators on appropriate timelines. With resource constraints and call for strong corporate governance and sustainability, the learning curve is steep for everyone as we may be starting from ground zero.

Trust building, especially trusting ourselves fully, will be required first.

These disruptions are not new, and neither is the rhetoric around change required. What is new is perhaps an awakening to a sense of collective power needed to surmount these challenges perhaps. Much of our personal and collective realities are driven by both external changes as much as our own inner worlds. Should we be in constant crisis mode, for instance? We need to look at it from a systems and individual perspective. Systems here can refer to the family units and organisational structures we are part of.

If we take time to step back from the chaos, we can start to acknowledge our roles and see how we receive and contribute to the feedback loops we create for ourselves and others. Perhaps in seeking equilibrium, we create chaos instead, which is more likely in the dynamic systems overlapping these days.[20] Understanding the role of positive feedback loops, how non-linear our systems are, and what is predictable and what can be easily solved will help lighten the load.

Harvard Business School introduced in the 1960s and 1970s the concept of strategic planning, which stressed the need to integrate standard business functions with a systematic approach to an overall strategy.[21] Reality shows us that highly mechanistic plans and mathematical forecasts do not always work. Massachusetts Institute of Technology (MIT) introduced system dynamics, which is equally risky and based on subjective assumptions and value judgements since it is also trying to judge what is ahead from what is going on in the back end.[22]

Simplistic modelling will not do either since we exist in a complex universe. Forecasting has to be a holistic and continuous process with feedback, sensitive dependence and non-linear developments kept firmly in view.[23] Social systems on the whole are not easy to understand due to their complexity and diversity. We may simply be experiencing warm temperatures as the global greenhouse effect undergoes its changes,

---

[20] S. Ziauddin and A. Iwona, *Introducing Chaos: A Graphic Guide*, London, Icon Books, 2004, pp. 152-153, **[e-book]**.

[21] Ziauddin and Iwona, *Introducing Chaos*, p. 211.

[22] Ziauddin and Iwona, *Introducing Chaos*, p. 212.

[23] Ziauddin and Iwona, *Introducing Chaos*, p. 220.

which is a series of warm winters and hot summers. It may not necessarily mean that long-term, permanent change has set in. We will need to ask sensible questions and stop making naive assumptions about the source of complexity or pattern.

We will need a new way of thinking about nature, the physical world, and ourselves.

What Is Stopping Us?

At the leadership, governance, and management levels, we need more vulnerability. It is at the core of transformational leadership just as much as empathy is. Gone are the days where top-down approaches of the leader who knows best can be accepted. As we evolve as a human race, the autonomy of self will only increase as our prowess to make change and innovate will only grow, depending on how quickly our systems in which we live adapt or suppress these changes. We need this to happen if we are going to achieve interconnected governance. This is the sharing of burdens otherwise disproportionately placed on governments (national, regional, local) to deal with tragedy of the commons, public goods, and emerging climate-related financial risks.

Interconnected leadership requires us to embrace our totality as a human—the seen and shadow side in order to effectively be whole and grounded. Figure 6 below shows the complexities in this approach, which we can start by accepting ourselves as imperfectly perfect. There is no more hiding or fear of others/opinions/expectations when we know all of ourselves and no longer fight it because someone told us in the past that this part of us was bad. Imagine, when we do not embrace our shadow side, it is forced to be in the background. When we switch to automatic or unconscious thinking mode, which happens throughout our day when we are doing routine tasks or just switched off or too wired up with an emotion, the shadow side gets a chance to be seen. If we truly want to self-reflect and know what is in our shadow, we can wait for people's feedback in the moment our shadows appear—you may notice their expressions, body language, or how they respond to you.

Often it might leave you feeling a little strange about what has happened, almost like something else took over you. Well, that is our shadow side trying to come in and have a say because, well, we have not allowed it to do so, so far. When we sit with these experiences, we start a dialogue with our shadow side instead, and we start to negotiate these expressions. We get to tell our shadow selves, 'I hear you, I see you, and I am sorry. How may we work through this part of ourselves I have shunned or shamed because someone told me that you are not right?' Through this process we can release displaced guilt and shame that was never ours to begin with in the first place. A stressed caregiver may have said something to us in anger, and we hid that part of us so that we will not experience that uncomfortable feeling again or feel like we were their reasons for stressing. This happens subtly, and as adults, professionals, we constantly give and receive interpersonal feedback. Daily reflections on what is happening in our lives instead of further distracting or draining our energy in activities to avoid this growth mindset will be helpful in the long run. We will be able to break out of harmful cycles where toxic work cultures develop.

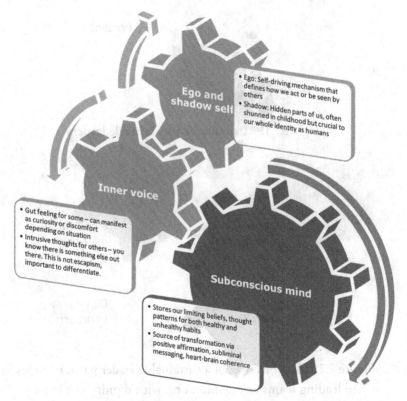

Figure 6: How we influence our own thoughts and actions

This is not to say we will completely do away with bad actors. They will remain in this universe for varied reasons, most times to remind us what is important and necessary in regulating harm to others. Nonetheless, the quicker we accelerate this self-leadership momentum towards interconnected governance, the sooner the multiplier effect can kick in at organisational and community levels. Outcome? Rise of sustainable leaders who are self-aware, grounded, and assured of their purpose in life, and who inspire and uplift others in the process of just being themselves. Figure 7 below details what to expect from sustainable leaders.

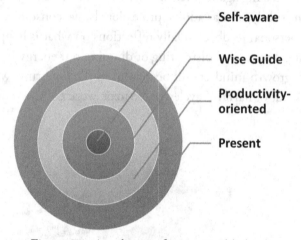

Figure 7.1: Attributes of a sustainable leader

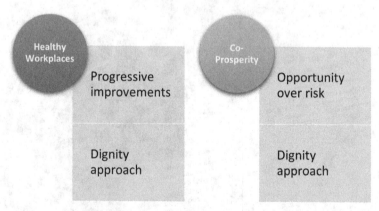

Figure 7.2: The objectives of a sustainable leader when it comes to leading teams or organisations, with dignity as a basis

Our systems are unfortunately built on shaky foundations and people leading them, vain (myself included). If we truly cared about sustainability, we would be further along. Instead, we remain in our respective echo chambers, and only a minority are cleaning up their act, with hopes that this movement will grow despite the lack of enablers currently. Climate policies are piecemeal and tricky given the competing socio-economic considerations as well as practical. It is not a popular time to be in policymaking or business sustainability. There are more questions than answers unless we start grounding ourselves.

Similar patterns exist across most systems—elite-driven decision-making from politics to where finance is allocated. Money politics and business-politics nexus create an unhealthy feedback system for change—it is in business and government's interest to maintain status quo as much as possible to maintain order and to live up to the next political cycle. Because self-preservation is our main obstacle, we do not realise how we too contribute to the system failures of our governance and societal systems. Often, we must co-opt to be recognised, fit in, and belong. This comes at the detriment of others who do not benefit from a system that continues to discriminate against them. Access is still limited to people with money or education or both.

Social cohesion and more importantly, peace is still missing in a lot of our communities with civil war, displacement of communities from climate, political, socio-economic crises as well as identity politics. Bridging and interfacing across different economies and communities can offer space for new ideas and cooperative values to transcend what are often historical and potentially outdated differences between people. Recognising the arguments of all, a certain detachment focusing on community upliftment will be needed. Much like with ideology, the setting aside of differences to agree to disagree needs to take place to negotiate peace on new terms.

Everywhere, the same issues of perpetual indifference to the disparities of our time prevail. Means testing or unemployment benefits do not help either, and neither do our charity or philanthropic efforts since it keeps the poor poor and rich richer. Just to assuage our egos or hearts that we are doing good by donating is irresponsible use of our hard-earned income and underestimation of the potential nonprofit or social enterprises can have to accelerate their respective theory of changes to enact a systemic shift.

Education unfortunately is becoming less of an enabler today as skills jump to the forefront. With many anxious about climate change, nature, approach to life, and pursuit of happiness are evolving for the younger generations. We need to adapt, and we are too big a problem to do so fast.

It is a known fact that groupthink exists in most cultures, largely because of fear and societal conditioning. It takes sheer courage and acceptance of our awareness to step out of boundaries with people we live, work, and love to live our true expression. As many autobiographies will show, this detachment is necessary in order to have the space to decondition and realise what we need to know about ourselves and our true North Star. Most of us are living lives and expectations of others just so we can be loved or feel that we belong. We already belong to ourselves, and that is more than enough. Time has a way of healing and bringing back more love into your life and meaningful relationships.

Therefore, the action gap is addressing each one of us. We know plastic pollution, for example, is a highly scalable pollution issue to the extent that microplastics are entering our bloodstreams. We might make the change to reusable bags but still actively source for and utilise consumables with packaging. It is too prevalent—we cannot avoid it, or can we? Also, there are stewards who know better and have wisdom from times before but are often not part of conversations because of our own biases and preferences to include only those whom we are comfortable or familiar with.

Even where affirmative actions may be made, prejudices are inherent. Most of us do not expect the other to *really* make a difference, as it might threaten us. Most of us are OK with the charade of hosting meetings, events and not truly effecting change substantively, year-on-year with clear impact metrics and theory of change. We claim alignments to various global commitments, which are nonetheless a good start. Change begins with normative stances before we can internalise, but do we have more time to waste?

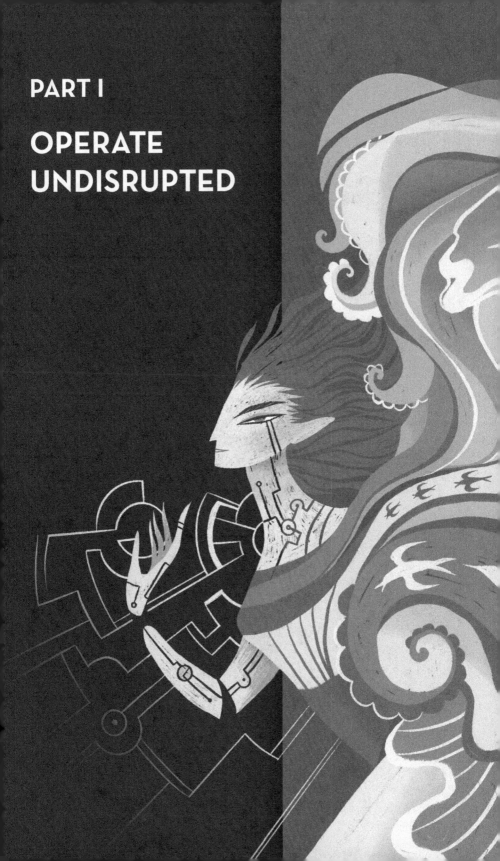

PART I

OPERATE
UNDISRUPTED

I

SEE THINGS AS THEY ARE

Business Sustainability in Asia

The most comprehensive textbook I have come across is *Business Sustainability in Asia: Compliance, Performance, and Integrated Reporting and Assurance*.[24] Unfortunately, most of its content has been updated given the heightened progress both regulators and corporations made because of the outcome of the 2020 COVID-19 global pandemic. Singapore's Green Plan 2030, for instance, was launched on 10 February 2021, showing how nascent many of the substantive normative and policy changes we hope to achieve in the near term are.

Nevertheless, the book captures the unvarying role of corporate governance in managing corporate affairs and activities for the benefit of its stakeholders such as shareholders, investors, board members, and other stakeholders via a network of monitoring and incentives, good corporate governance, transparency in order to achieve increase capital inflows.[25] This largely depends on the organisational culture resulting from the

---

[24]   Z. Rezaee, J. Tsui P. Cheng and G. Zhou, *Business Sustainability in Asia: Compliance, Performance, and Integrated Reporting and Assurance*, London, John Wiley and Sons, 2019.

[25]   Rezaee, Tsui P and Zhou, *Business Sustainability in Asia*, p.164, pp.171-5.

tone management sets and the integrity of employees as well as corporate governance mechanisms that encourage improvements in transparency and disclosures.[26]

With a strategic focus on sustainability, businesses can build resilience within the organisation and in markets to improve both efficiency and economic prosperity, if they want to. Chapter 6, 'Co-Prosperity as a Value', argues that this value creation and alignment might be a business imperative if we truly want to achieve our net-zero, nature-positive goals.

Switching to Regenerative Systems

Regeneration requires acknowledgement of dignity at its core. This acceptance that just as we are valuable and worthy of access to natural resources and their many by-products, so are fellow human beings in the present and future. In imbuing this right, we can exercise it in different ways that can bring about profound change. Chapter 2, 'Overcome Powerlessness', uncovers our universal challenge in change management and how to persist through what seems impossible to break through.

In owning dignity as a human, we understand the need for due diligence to properly guide us in our discernment of how we use resources available to us. This may come in the form of product quality checklists, supplier vendor risk assessments, consumer opinion polling, market research, as well as related compliance standards. With knowing what scope and measures we could consider in ensuring dignity remains integral to how we function, we can start to invite collective wisdom to percolate in our intelligence systems.

Intelligence here refers to wisdom from our frontline workers, the communities in which we operate in, the loyal consumers and their insights. This would enrich our institutional databases and ensure our knowledge work is shape-shifting with local systems of thought. This information we can gather without cost and with a keen sense of gratitude for the constant feedback loops that otherwise go amiss.

---

[26]   Rezaee, Tsui P and Zhou, *Business Sustainability in Asia,* pp. 180-81, 191, 220, 269.

Gratitude also opens us to a state of receptivity, which is crucial if we want to keep our businesses relevant and relatable to mass markets. There is a lot that needs to be churned through and this can come with sufficient data mining systems with customised curation to reach the pulse of the market. When we have this subtle information, we can go on to nurture our systems of work further in more substantive and authentic ways. The goal here is to build a formidable system of trust and authenticity for all stakeholders to engage and contribute to resilience.

The COVID-19 pandemic saw the closure of many businesses around the world. Those who had community backing managed to stay afloat longer, and those with resilience planning survived. Chapter 4, 'Who Is Important', helps us work through our own stakeholder lists and priority engagements to build long-standing trust.

There is no one-size-fits-all answer, and it is OK. We just need to build sustainably (within our means), and this comes with ensuring we stay illuminated through the process with stakeholder engagement, relevant feedback loops, and state of receptivity to internalise and shape-shift to the next business cycle. Staying fixed in one structure is no longer helpful as business disruptions are ad hoc and sporadic in nature, with emerging risks largely unknown despite the best guesswork by experts and economic modelling. Staying close to the ground while being aware of macro developments is how we may secure tangible outcomes in our sustainability efforts.

Tangible here refers to trust and resilience, which are not quantified yet in various ESG metrics. Besides carbon, energy, waste, water and various occupational health and safety (OHS), social and governance metrics, the need to consider their overall impact score on business and community resilience is helpful. Chapter 3, 'Own What We Can Know', details this further.

With strong trust and resilience, we can be assured that our yield on investment returns will be recurring despite downturns and market rebounds. This would be the true benefits of a regenerative system built with nature and community in mind.

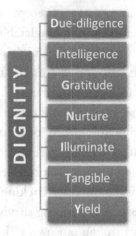

Figure 8: Seven key benefits of embedding dignity®

However, this may be a far leap from where we are currently at. Are we considering how to create regenerative cycles of production? Not at scale. Instead, we might be displacing an unsustainable component with a more sustainable resource such as ethanol in biofuel, to claim a transition is happening. Whether the output will be lower in carbon consumption across its product life cycle is left to be seen as it completes its process. We are therefore still market-facing and market-driven, and these quick-fix approaches, albeit with much investment of research and development as well as time and resources, require more application and time to test-bed further. Why create anew though when ancient wisdom shares living more sustainably in key?

Regenerative focus and shifts need to impart dignity for all. It is important to avoid commoditising aspects of nature in order to safeguard it. Establishing nature as its own asset class is good in ensuring biodiversity loss is curbed but not if we are going to pit it against another commodity and trade. The stock markets of our world have only shown how vulnerable they are to investment flows and analyst opinions. Subjecting the care of nature to these market mechanisms is detrimental, to say the least, and we are being forewarned.

Dignity and systems thinking can help by identifying the different enablers both upstream and downstream and where the intervention points are in transitioning an existing linear system of take and make to a regenerative, circular one.

Figure 9 details the thought process besides awareness. Organisations will need appropriate knowledge and know-how to transition towards a low-carbon, greener future. Businesses are well placed to decarbonise by approaching carbon neutrality first and then net zero followed by net positive or nature positive. Understandably this takes time and partnerships, and we can get started with the initial steps by procuring the information we need in understanding our respective business revenue streams, financial risk relating to disruptions such as extreme weather patterns, supply chain delays, and public health scares.

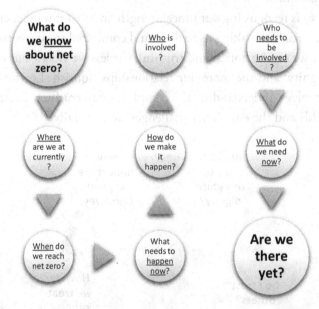

Figure 9: Sense-making where we are at in our decarbonisation journey

Technology may help us understand the scale of our business problems; however, it is not the answer. People are. When there is trust and transformative leadership across our legal systems, culture, and politics, we all thrive. From frontline staff to contracted workers, doing the right thing is empowering all, no matter the knowledge and skills level, to lead as effectively as possible to drive innovation, positive change at all levels in order to derive greater organisational impact. This is often stifled by culture, management styles, self-beliefs, which will require honest and enabling conversations. Also, according to Dr Donna Hicks, 'most people do not have a working knowledge of dignity'. As a result, they are unaware of both their own inherent value and worth as well as how to recognise it in another.[27]

When we are aware of how to treat ourselves and others in a way that shows they matter, we are more empowered by dignity.[28] This is different from respect. We are all born with dignity, while respect is something we earn along the way from what we do. And when we violate others by how we treat them, this power can be destructive, cause emotional tension, and break trust between people. When we honour one another, we feel safe and free to be vulnerable and to be our true selves because we are seen, heard, and valued.[29]

Dignity is recognising our inner strength and that it is independent of how others treat us, making us resilient and connected to our worthiness.[30] 'The more we can be honest and truthful, the less we violate our own and others' dignity, and the more our relationships flourish. Learning about dignity involves understanding the complex, often conflicted state of our inner worlds and the emotional challenges we face daily'.[31]

Figure 10: Leader's self-reflection wheel

27   D. Hicks, *Leading with Dignity: How to Create a Culture That Brings Out the Best in People,* New Haven, Yale University Press, 2018, p.10, [**e-book**].

28   Hicks, *Leading with Dignity,* p.11.

29   Hicks, *Leading with Dignity,* pp.80-1.

30   Hicks, *Leading with Dignity,* p. 55.

31   Hicks, *Leading with Dignity,* pp. 41-2.

Honing dignity in leadership failures illuminates blind spots; it helps us become critical thinkers and embrace a new approach to conflict resolution.[32] The dignity® approach also encourages us to embrace interdependence through feedback from others on our own blind spots by sharing, listening, and being aware of one another's feelings and including others.[33] We can be effective as polite when it comes to creating generative cultures at our workplaces. This requires understanding our shared humanity, creating space for vulnerability, providing strong values-based and ethical leadership approaches. Chapter 5, 'Leaders Who Succeed', provides insights on the ethical code of conduct required for collective success.

Values such as promoting transparency, practising ethical conduct, providing fair judgement by respecting and reciprocating to achieve committed action and timely professional delivery, will be required. Figure 11 below provides a visualisation of this process.

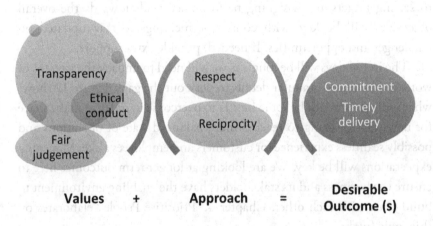

Values + Approach = Desirable Outcome (s)

Figure 11: Ideal model for harmonious and progressive working relationships

In an ever increasingly interconnected world today, an individual action has a consequence on another. By exercising critical thinking, we can unlock the biases and limited mental models that could be inhibiting

32 D. Hicks, *Leading with Dignity: How to Create a Culture That Brings Out the Best in People*, New Haven, Yale University Press, 2018, p. 51, [**e-book**].
33 Hicks, *Leading with Dignity*, p. 87.

us from truly connecting with another.[34] As mentioned in the introduction, we will need to navigate our own ego, inner world, and shadow self as well as subconscious mind.

How we choose to show up daily to our own lives and interact with others matters, and how others do so with us is important as well. Much of the stress and turmoil existing in the world today is self-created, which we can transmute with a values-based approach to working with each other and ensuring the foundations we build are solid for future generations to stand upon. Much is at risk if we remain stagnant or flippant with this discourse. We would be building in linear ways, disregarding the opportunities to optimise resources and achieve savings on other metrics that can bring about a healthier planet for all.

The transition starts with awareness and simple tricks to make the shifts. These shifts need not be large, overwhelming ones, just quantum leaps consistently. For larger organisations, carrot-and-stick approaches to setting targets and assigning performance goals towards the overall objectives will be key, with consistent meetings to stay updated on challenges and opportunities. If needed, provide extra support.

The initial days will be tough as we will need to unpack the streams of work and look into granular details to sieve out the gaps. Figure 12 shows what indicators might be some inertia to overcome in order to make space for new ways of being to reach a more balanced state of operations and possibly seamless experience for customers and employees alike. Managing expectations will be key. We are looking at longer-term outcomes here to ensure the business and its stakeholders have the enabling environment to build trust with each other. Chapter 4, 'Prioritise People', elaborates on this topic further.

---

[34]   D. Hicks, *Leading with Dignity: How to Create a Culture That Brings Out the Best in People,* New Haven, Yale University Press, 2018, p. 92, **[e-book]**.

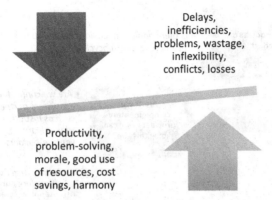

Figure 12: Ideas for organisations to reach a balanced state of operations

Sustainability is increasingly growing in its depth for corporate reporters as regulators and public goods face resource and financial challenges from emerging and forecasted climate risks along with its associated sociopolitical challenges.

Allies will be important. Once we know and accept that we need others to be sustainable together, we can start mapping the opportunities. Ecosystem mapping to encourage more effective behavioural change with suitable incentive schemes that help businesses achieve more footfall and positively impact the environment will be required. It is still too convenient to take-make-waste than it is to reduce-reuse-recycle these days.

Partnering with start-ups, charities, waste management firms, especially those serving complementary needs to the business line, will grow increasingly necessary. Employees, supply chain, and consumers will be important as well. First line of defence will always be frontline managers, who make the best reporters and advocates for sustainability issues as they know the business operations in-depth. Second line will be suppliers, whom we will need to keep engaging to ensure they are aware of business needs to grow sustainability and how everyone can do their part, especially with new ideas. Lastly, consumers and what role they can play in reducing waste or ensuring the product moves from cradle-to-gate to cradle-to-grave. The responsibility for end-of-life assurance needs to fall on both the seller and buyer with proper awareness of possibilities to upcycle, recycle, reuse, reduce before reaching the landfill. The figure below illustrates some key thought-processes in implementing this approach.

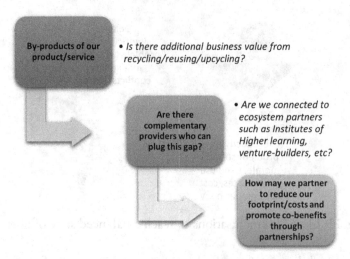

Figure 13: Considering adjacent new possibilities for resource optimisation with new partners

Paradigms That Hold Us Back

Dr Tasha Eurich's research compiled in her book *Insight* describes self-awareness as the meta-skill for the twenty-first century, and she defines it as 'the ability to see ourselves clearly—to understand who we are, how others see us and how we fit into the world around us'. She elaborates further that 'there is strong scientific evidence that people who know themselves and how others see them are happier. They make smarter decisions. They have better personal and professional relationships. They raise more mature children. They are smarter, superior students who choose better careers. They are more creative, more confident, and better communicators. They are less aggressive and less likely to lie, cheat and steal. They're better performers at work who get more promotions. They are more effective leaders with more enthusiastic employers. They even lead more profitable companies.'

Eurich argues 'self-delusion', which is the opposite of self-awareness, is a more common issue though and sometimes mistaken as insight. This is because, in reality, self-awareness is a remarkably rare quality. She reviews the importance of emotional intelligence (EQ) in self-assessments. EQ tends to be problematic because it may not accurately reflect what we really are, based on how we see ourselves. A likely increase in EQ could relate to a decrease in self-awareness.

Eurich shares that internal self-awareness is 'an inward understanding of your **values** (the principles that guide them), **passions** (what they love to do), **aspirations** (what they want to experience and achieve), **ideal environment** (the environment they require to be happy and engaged), **patterns** (consistent ways of thinking, feeling and behaving), **reactions** (the thoughts, feelings, and behaviours that reveal their capabilities), and **impact** on others'. Seeing yourself clearly in this regard ensures you make choices aligned with what makes you truly happy and satisfied.

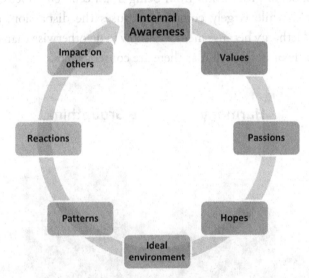

Figure 14: Internal awareness can illuminate most of our struggles to ourselves without any interventions

This is why the sooner we realise the known/unknown neurotic anxieties that plague us all, the sooner we release ourselves from the mind jails we have put ourselves into, thinking this is the be-all and end-all, and that we *have* to escape, take flight, hide. Of course, with toxic environments, it is important to throw light on the toxicity and make clear boundaries. If it proves too challenging: leave, forgive, heal, and believe in attracting better opportunities. It is when we do not believe we are worthy of better opportunities that we attract the same types of experiences again. The pattern repeats until we resolve it.

To see things as they are would require working with current reality as an ally according to Peter Senge in his book *The Fifth Discipline*. By learning how to interpret and co-create with change rather than resist it. By being deeply inquisitive to see more of reality unfolding, with accuracy. Most importantly, by upholding a high level of personal mastery to continuously learn and develop physical and intellectual abilities as much as emotional.

There is no doubt that power is strongest when consolidated and centralised. With a strong command centre and helicopter view of what is happening around us, quicker decisions can be made by an elite few on behalf of broader society. The issue with such a system is when there are blind spots or groupthink from being in an echo chamber or reality. Groupthink, while largely compliant, causes the dispassion, stagnant energy, and lethargy because members know to do otherwise than expected is either futile or not worth it as there are consequences.

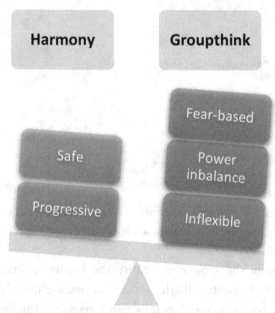

Figure 15: Groupthink presents itself as fabricated harmony, taking us further away from authentic harmony

How we may untangle ourselves from this requires an earnest questioning attitude to everything we do and ensuring the North Star remains in clear view for purpose-driven leaders.

Yet this approach is sidelined for various personal or collective agendas or time pressures. Often self-preservation is at the core of this issue. If we question, 'authorities' may feel disrespected, threatened, or demoralised. Rather than allowing this to happen, transparency and consultation are managed to avoid over-engagement and/or disclosure. The cost-benefit analysis of such an approach is clear—to save time and effort, it is best to decide what information is shared and with whom to get to the quickest or affirmative action required. And because we are human, the tendency to consult others remains in our closest circles or what we are comfortable to engage with, and information shared comes from a paternalistic perspective in that it is better you only know so much.

To effectively move forward, we cannot limit ourselves and the communities we work in any more. We must have the courage to self-reflect and know when something better can be done or needs to be done for the greater good. Our values need to reflect the changing times, and we need to get comfortable with the uncomfortable. Change has always been a constant. Each day, we are all ageing whether we like it or not. What we can do about it when we accept it varies drastically from when we reject this fact. With such a simple example, we can see the perils in how we have been communicating so far—within limited circles, often echo chambers or the converted to lack of transparency in fears of being vulnerable.

Our self-worth projected outwardly in the form of credibility need not be compromised in crisis if we know how to embrace change, imperfections, and vulnerability. To assume we know best or better is destabilising and to hold on to this facade is akin to manifesting a glass menagerie, where we get more dissociated from each other. In today's cost-of-living crises around the world, we cannot afford to lead and live this way anymore. Furthermore, vulnerability has been found to be a key shifting factor that allows 'a group to move into deeper resonance with each other to achieve more profound level of healing, community and creation'.[35]

---

[35]   A. Briskin, S. Erickson, T. Callanan J. Ott, *The Power of Collective Wisdom: And the Trap of Collective Folly*, San Francisco, Berrett-Koehler Publishers, 2009, p. 186, [**e-book**].

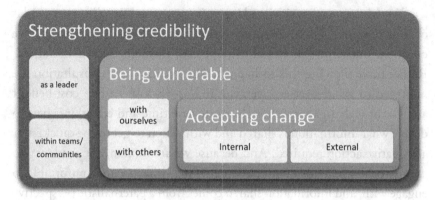

Figure 16: The value proposition of embracing a healthy relationship
between change, vulnerability, and building our self-worth

These illusions remain only because power and visibility flow in a
positive loop. The more power, the more visible; the more visible, the more
power one gets regardless of whether the impact one is creating is real or
not. If you are an engineer working remotely or a teacher in a far-flung
village with limited resources, the motivation to do your job and do it well
is less if one is in the command centres within respective headquarters
with direct access or resources. Those who still show up and build their
communities (and there are many unsung heroes who do) do so from
a values-based approach that our current market systems would peg as
intangible to measure and therefore compensate when these are the actual
objectives and key results driving the change much needed for innovation
and social mobility.

With accessibility being such an impediment to bridging the inequality
gap, it is therefore crucial we rethink the power structures we operate in.
And the time is upon us as global leaders fuel this conversation with
proposed restructuring from economist Minouche Shafik, formerly of
the International Monetary Fund (IMF), to the Bridgetown Initiative led
by Prime Minister Mia Mottley.[36] Social movements and coalitions even

---

[36]   S. Minouche, *What We Owe Each Other: A New Social Contract for a Better
       Society,* New Jersey, Princeton University Press, 2021; K. Liao, *What is the
       Bridgetown Initiative? What to know about the game-changing plan for climate
       finance,* Global Citizen, 9 May 2023, https://www.globalcitizen.org/en/content/
       climate-change-bridgetown-initiative-mia-mottley/ (accessed 26 January 2024).

in the private sector have grown through the course of 2021 through to present times to innovate, transform, and consider plausible futures where we collectively contribute to better and hopefully more just outcomes.

How To Embed Sustainability Into Our Systems

Sustainability is complex; it involves many different stakeholders, data points, and system operations. At any one time, unpredictability can set in. Take safety at the workplace for instance: minor and major injury rate control needs to be managed via a multi-prong approach including regular and updated risk assessments, internal audits, compliance meetings, Environmental, Health, Safety (EHS) advisories, random spot checks as well as daily reminders on and off site, depending on type of industry. Even then, human error or negligence can ensue, along with unnatural events such as a sudden onset of illness.

With such complexity, we need to embrace it rather than avoid it. We can also set up the remediation mechanisms to fast-track the response rate and keep adapting our systems with new features to prevent future exposure to 'increased risks or unwanted behaviours'.[37] It will be impossible to build a complete mental model since behaviour is unpredictable and nonlinear; however, by uncovering our system weaknesses that could impede our future growth and raise shareholder concerns, we will be better empowered by sustainability rather than overwhelmed.

I believe we can take a page from chaos engineering. This refers to the study of experiments undertaken to make systems stronger against drastic changes in operations.[38] Here the solution is not important, rather the goal along with the process, communication, and task management to ensure teams can be high-performance.[39]

---

[37] C. Rosenthal and N. Jones, *Chaos Engineering: System Resiliency in Practice,* California, O'Reilly Media, 2020, p.64, **[e-book]**.

[38] Rosenthal and Jones, *Chaos Engineering,* p. 393.

[39] Rosenthal and Jones, *Chaos Engineering,* pp. 17-8.

Step	Process	Objective
1	Identify existing systems and how sustainability metrics that show normal statistical performance or trend measured. This will be defined as the steady state, the state in which variables do not change over time.	To align on operational scope, process, and expected data outputs in a non-event situation
2	Establish a control group and an experiment group to assume the steady state as the starting point of their investigation	To see if experiments will affect any variable under the steady state
3	Introduce variables that reflect real-world events such as supply chain disruptions or rising resource costs, infrastructure damage from extreme weather patterns like flooding, transportation breakdown affecting commute, heat stress for outdoor workers, data breaches, etc.	To mimic plausible future scenarios that could impact operational resiliency and previously assumed in the steady state
4	Attempt to correct the hypothesis by looking for a difference in steady state between the control group and the experimental group	To have sufficient confidence in how the system behaves, to identify areas of improvement and rectify before they escalate[40]

Table 1: Implementing chaos engineering in systems improvement to achieve sustainability across an organisation

Experimentation will either build confidence or teach us new properties about our own system through verification of the output at a system boundary, validation of the parts of the system and mental models to reflect the interaction of those parts, and care about whether a system works or not.[41] Every organisation has resource cost considerations, workload limits, and information requirements to avoid safety incidents. An ideal system will not cross the boundary of economics/workload/safety margin, where the rubber band could snap.[42]

---

[40] C. Rosenthal and N. Jones, *Chaos Engineering: System Resiliency in Practice*, California, O'Reilly Media, 2020, p.64, **[e-book]**.

[41] Rosenthal and Jones, *Chaos Engineering*, pp. 85-6.

[42] Rosenthal and Jones, *Chaos Engineering*, p.67.

We need to be open to unexpected consequences and to practise recovery as best as we can. Resilience is created by people who 'dig deeper to find underlying risks and refine mental models of how our systems succeed and fail'.[43]

Shifting to collective mode

Systems theory emerged in the 1950s and is about how 'our universe is comprised of different types of systems—open, closed or isolated—and different scales of systems'.[44] It is grounded historically in the search for an understanding of all systems regardless of discipline since there are similarities in how different systems are structured and operated. Future-forward leaders are system thinkers regardless of their organisational boundaries. They are aware of the competing pressures surrounding their ecosystem and can think quickly, act rationally, and lead effectively on what it takes to address a problem when it emerges. By studying patterns, being part of networks, and influencing the systems we function in, system thinkers believe the whole is greater than the sum of its parts.

Systems are however unpredictable, non-linear, living, and organic, and understanding differences between systems ensures we understand the nuances from which we need to operate. Global and thematic databases offer insight regarding this systemic interplay, while bottom-up and context-specific internal databases covering your team's needs will also be required to ensure there is synchronicity and sense-making between databases to create new value.

This is where I am reminded of praxis in theatre, where through improvisation, ideas get heard, acted out, improvised. All the world is made up of constellations of engagement. If we just stop to be more mindful, we can see how we each contribute and grow the narratives within our own minds and communities. Often, we may hold on to dogmatic thinking

---

43   Rosenthal and Jones, *Chaos Engineering*, p. 262 **[e-book]**.

44   D. Straussfogel and C. von Schilling, 2009, Systems Theory. *International Encyclopaedia of Human Geography*, pp. 151–58, https://www.sciencedirect.com/science/article/abs/pii/B9780080449104007549 (accessed 26 January 2024).

and not realise the fear is coming from within us or the need to feel safe by exhibiting control is coming within us. Instead, we must take a page from theatre or the arts, where the negotiation and renegotiation of space, thought, and form is constantly worked on to eventually create a masterpiece that symbiotically weaves a master narrative through the exercise. This narrative, a cumulative experience, is both fleeting and transcendental in that notions of you and I merge, and identities converge to form anew. There is no distinction between whose idea is which but a bringing together of organic thoughts.

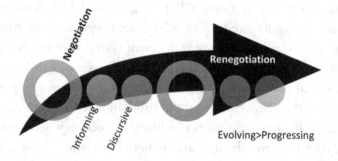

Figure 17: Human systems and leadership are a consistent practice of negotiation and renegotiation of what our environments feed back to us and how we respond to them

Operating from a strengths approach is crucial as we move forward. Having access and gaining direct inputs from stakeholders as well as offering verified information to stakeholders especially in terms of crisis communications or public service campaigns will become increasingly crucial as we digitise more and more, with heightened cybersecurity risks and misinformation- or disinformation-related issues.

Ideally this new form of engagement with machine- and human-centred approach creates new team positions focusing on better integration of data with customer profile/needs. Integrated workflows and deeper insights could build stronger bridges between communities and governance institutions. And stronger communities are driven primarily by their businesses and market systems. Understanding this interconnection and the evolving role of businesses will quicken internal transitions towards stronger customer experience management, for business viability in the mid to long term.

Building emotional design is even more important as the world addresses issues of climate change, gender inequality, market failures, and public health crises like the COVID-19 pandemic, to name a few.

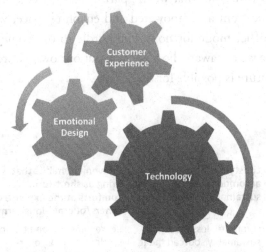

Figure 18: The interplay of technology, with appropriate emotional design to enhance customer experience will be key in business 4.0

These issues are cross-cutting and intersectional, impacting all areas of business development, from HR to operations. As such, recognising how businesses communicate these issues in relation to the service they offer is becoming increasingly crucial and healthy as we move forward towards a more interconnected world, thanks to progressive connectivity advancements. Co-designing integration in workflows, be it with AI or local communities, also offers cross-pollinating solutions to manifest itself.

These tensions are showing us the fissures within our societies so that we can find ways to heal them. Competition and conflict do not help, and neither do our methods of sabotaging a process towards common ground with our own perceptions and fears: 'Conflict can be an invitation for a higher order of resolution (including) . . . listening, deciphering and unlocking new alternatives (by) . . . understanding the situation and grasping the basic needs of all those involved'.[45]

---

[45]   A. Briskin, S. Erickson, J. Ott and T. Callanan; *The Power of Collective Wisdom: And the Trap of Collective Folly*, San Francisco, Berrett-Koehler Publishers, 2009, p.286, [e-book].

Every day, each one of us is contributing to the carbon footprint on earth, for example, yet we feel apart from the system. This can change once we start noticing that small steps can add up and the responsibility to act starts with us and that we are part of a larger community. Again, this must come from an empowered and enabling space, when we exist mainly in conflict mode for now. The hurdle to overcome now is what do we do once we are aware, how we may put our own swords down, and what better future is possible for us.

Lifestyle changes to accomodate more sustainable choices	Convenient habits that bring us short-term comforts at the expense of others/our mid-long term
i.e. hybrid cooling, green commute, less meat or sustainably sourced meat, more movement and social connections, etc	i.e. regular air-conditioning, single-use items, over-consumption, food waste, fast-fashion, frequent flyer, etc

Figure 19: Small changes can help reduce our carbon footprint

What Are We Sustaining?

Business bottom lines are undeniably triple these days. To make enduring profits, we are dependent on people and the planet.

Today's business leader needs to be some form of a community-builder or at least have a vision for collective progress. Given the types of crises that are emerging, it pays more dividends to invest in building more networks and more sustainable leaders within the business to stand strong against market challenges. And every stakeholder counts in managing our resource ownership better.

Here discernment is important, and we can learn to enhance it. How do we see the situation as it is, not how we want it to be? How do we receive complete information, or do we have doubts that we may not have sufficient information? Where may we seek clarifications, or are clarifications not allowed? And if something needs to be said, is it safe to say? These are red-flag questions when figuring out first if we may be able to discern accurately. Most times, information is controlled or presented in a limited manner in order to shape certain lines of thinking or narratives. It is not necessary to unearth these hidden agendas; however, knowing the extent we may accurately understand others and the situation will be helpful. Where there are many red flags, we know to trust our inner instincts more than what we see and hear. And where indiscernible, either ask for more information when it is safe or step aside completely. Not all environments are suited for us, and we do not need to fight all battles.

In addition to these red flags, there might be inherent challenges to fully comprehend the urgent need to act responsibly coupled with distractions and lack of follow-through or over-following through for some of us, we may hit roadblocks. Managing our expectations will be key when we start to see these realities as they are. They are not necessarily bad. Progress can still be made when we understand their root causes.

Trust and safety will be key here, learning to reframe negative situations, thinking from a neutral mind, and reaching common ground with others to grow our interdependence: 'This begins with a conscious intention to seek out what might work for all even when the path seems blocked or strewn with obstacles'.[46] By acknowledging the human in each other, we activate a field of engagement for compassion to come through to generate constructive learning strategies stemming from our inherent differences. Certainty is not guaranteed, and we suspend it to seek common ground instead. This way we can shift towards the collective realisation that 'the situation will not change unless *we change*'.[47]

---

[46] A. Briskin, S. Erickson, J. Ott and T. Callanan; *The Power of Collective Wisdom: And the Trap of Collective Folly*, San Francisco, Berrett-Koehler Publishers, 2009, p. 290, **[e-book]**.

[47] A. Briskin, S. Erickson, J. Ott and T. Callanan; *The Power of Collective Wisdom*, p. 290.

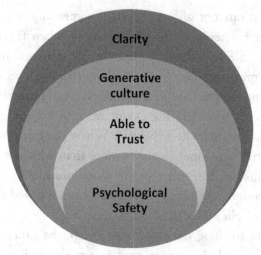

Figure 20: The best state to discern requires complete clarity, which comes to be when our environments are open, honest, and trust-building

By sharing power, seeing each other as equals, and accepting uncertainty, conflict resolution and problem-solving are achievable. For businesses, focusing on the consumer has always been a proven business tactic. With heightened regulatory push towards sustainability disclosures, more stakeholders need to be included, especially local communities impacted upstream and downstream across business operations. Community growth, building, and upliftment require ethnographic studies and evidence-based findings, which can be hard to fund or difficult to track the more geospatially remote we go. However, the initial investment is crucial as no business is isolated from the impacts it creates, be it via its secondary suppliers or direct business operations: 'Weave and the thread will follow'.[48]

A Values-Based Approach

When we pursue sustainability, we start to embody a belief system that we are not separate from others and that our actions have an impact on another. In fact, groups with strong sense of belonging and nurturing

---

[48]   A. Briskin, S. Erickson, J. Ott and T. Callanan; *The Power of Collective Wisdom*, p. 294, [e-book].

relationships can be their own source of empowerment.[49] Also, we view the world from disparate lenses of interconnected factors. This is a rare ability given our structure-agency frameworks have been bounded in silo thinking, whether intentional or unintentional. Built for one purpose, we need to see how we are complementary to another to create new value.

Think tanks, for example, are constantly ideating and developing new concepts and plausible solutions to the crisis of our times. Yet the linkage between their work and that of corporations is missing. To become a research practitioner, someone who is not just academically inclined but also experiments with real-life case studies, not to fit one's theory but to really evaluate its feasibility, needs to start happening. For this, institutions need to give these bright minds the space and connections to co-create systemic change with other organisations. This would be the think tank of the future.

How then do we get comfortable with what scares us? Despite being at a more advanced level of development compared to the industrial age, we still think, feel, and behave with our most basic instincts—those of survival and defence.

In today's world, where the rights of others are denied through continued war, discrimination, and socio-economic upheaval, the space for empowered action remains liminal. The morally right approach and business imperative therefore needs to be a values-based one. How we retain our self-identity and emancipate ourselves at the same time is at the crux of this. From economic empowerment, we can grow the human potential even more, if we want.

For corporate reporters, 2023 has seen much progress in sustainability disclosure from a business resilience standpoint as well as corporate social responsibility perspective. Yet it remains daunting as multiple stakeholders, especially different business functions, need to understand and integrate the updates into their workflows. Business practices need to adapt, and data adequately captured, tracked and, reported. The sooner we all understand this, the faster we pivot and welcome innovation in our business models, procurement and engagement. This does not mean we need to understand

---

49   A. Briskin, S. Erickson, J. Ott and T. Callanan; *The Power of Collective Wisdom*, p. 38 [e-book].

the whole gambit of what is out in the ecosystem. This book breaks it down for you.

For starters, it is good to know that most markets require listed companies to provide sustainability reports. The comprehensiveness and brevity vary, with the Singapore Stock Exchange leveraging a technology platform that splits core from comprehensive reporting to ensure baseline material non-financial data is at least disclosed. Now how much gets disclosed is up to the company, be it equity or operational control, and jurisdictions may be included or excluded, unless in the European Union. After submitting an annual report like the annual report, the cycle repeats. This need not be two separate reports going forward.

And in my opinion, one report stream is the way to go. Investors and customers, as well as staff and prospective talents can understand the sustainable business model through one report. This is different from a traditional annual report with a CSR section or year-on-year trends analysis on energy, water, waste, carbon data or the Enterprise Risk Management furnishing some details on climate-related risk mitigation and adaptation.

This will require an optimisation of how we procure to how we run our organisations to downstream objectives such as end-of-life processing. Some strategies include product life extension, remanufacturing or resource recovery to avoid procuring new virgin materials, and optimising waste as a resource. Product as a service model and/or sharing platforms like marketplaces to bring both buyers and sellers into one space as well as to share inventory without needing to own as many capital assets or real estate. Repair and resell goods that are still in good condition.

A company's impact on the environment and society is as important as the environment's financial impact on the company. A circular economy where we limit the use of virgin materials and optimise our existing resources to future-proof by diverting resources that can still be used and innovate certain processes to encourage a healthy feedback loop is beneficial as cost and environmental savings. Avoiding emissions besides scope 1, 2, and 3 or direct and indirect greenhouse gas (GHG) emissions needs to be our accounting metric for this. Till then, creating new business value or reducing cost savings has made the business case for transitioning.

How to Proceed: Double Materiality

Competitive advantage is still largely carved out by lower operating costs and therefore lower prices for consumers. It is also tough to incorporate sustainability values into a conventional business especially if managers are chasing quarterly targets.[50] However, with some businesses where dropping price is not an option or in its values, like for cooperatives supporting family-owned businesses, the adoption of sustainability can be a crucible of change towards building trust and extending one's responsibility towards the environment and society, which can also be its competitive advantage when recessions are not guiding consumers towards low-priced options.

It is therefore important to define the core issues that matter most to a company's stakeholders and consumers, followed by how progress will be measured. With tangible indicators, a competitor analysis would be helpful in motivating managers to outdo immediate rivals. Lastly, by starting with one business unit, other business units can see the benefits and scale up the impact eventually. However, if these efforts are not communicated well, companies can lose out on the chance to build both brand and trust with their consumers. This was the case in the early 2000s with Marks & Spencer, who invested millions of pounds to operate sustainably compared to its low-price competitors like Tesco and Wal-Mart but had not communicated these efforts to its value chain until they launched Look Behind the Label, a twelve-month ad campaign.[51]

The year 2023 saw the official launch of international sustainability reporting standards by the International Sustainability Standards Board (ISSB) initially established at COP26 meetings in Glasgow by the International Financial Reporting Standards (IFRS). The intention behind this movement is monumental—how may we report environmental and social data within conventional financial frameworks and how may we consolidate various mainstream frameworks under one framework? This mammoth task that began in November 2021

---

50   J. Hollender and B. Breen, *The Responsibility Revolution: How the Next Generation of Businesses Will Win*, San Francisco, Jossey-Bass, 2010, p.198, [**e-book**].

51   Hollender and Breen, *The Responsibility Revolution*, p.142.

concluded with the launch of two new frameworks—IFRS S1 and S2—on 26 June 2023.

It is not important to know the historical development of how this standard came to be; neither should it overwhelm us. Put simply, it has merged key components of various frameworks (TCFD, CDSB, VRF) and standards (namely GRI and SASB) to simplify non-financial disclosure in two different documentation—S1 and S2. The ISSB also only focuses on single materiality—which is financial and how climate change impacts the company.[52] The main audience here are investors. Double materiality is mainly legislated in Europe. Meant for a multi-stakeholder audience, it looks at both positive and negative impact on people and the environment over the short, medium, and long term.

Most of our common challenges when we embark on sustainability include confusion and lack of know-how on what to prioritise. Because it is as much an internal exercise as it is external, the priority ought to be internal first—sorting out the relevant regulations and compliance standards needed to adhere to, followed by what will it take for us to get there. This is where an ESG strategy that works hand in hand with business strategy will be useful, followed by a materiality study on what our stakeholders identify as significant business impact, risks, and opportunities. This will provide us with the prioritisation framework we need to gather relevant data to manage our ESG performance and report to our stakeholders.

Science-based targets, ESG scoring, GHG inventory are good to have but not the core. It will distract a small business, for instance, from achieving tangible savings from its sustainability efforts as well as identifying opportunities for innovation. Once a consistent journey has begun, the reporting cycle can follow with appropriate communications to key stakeholders. Technology may not be helpful especially if it is not clearly engaging the relevant personnel. Ideally, a digital platform should save time and increase productivity of workers to ensure returns on investment (ROI) are optimised.

---

[52]   Deloitte, *The Challenge of Double Materiality Sustainability Reporting at a Crossroad*, https://www2.deloitte.com/cn/en/pages/hot-topics/topics/climate-and-sustainability/dcca/thought-leadership/the-challenge-of-double-materiality.html(accessed 26 January 2024).

This means technology is an integrated part of everyone's workflow, whereby traceability and accuracy can be upheld. It will be intuitive as it is automated and, more importantly, decision-useful. As we are still digitally transitioning, the sophistication of enterprise tools is also growing. COVID-19 has greatly accelerated many features' development as well as promise for technology to be a level playing field for all of us especially in the knowledge sector with generative artificial intelligence, learning management systems, and big data.

There is hence no doubt about our increasing interconnectedness regarding how we operate in our private and public lives, as well as how we engage and impact environmental, social, and governance aspects of our lives. The sustainability lens lends us a circular, closed-loop, regenerative approach to living which far transcends our current ways of consumption and functioning in this world. To amplify business action especially in mobilising private capital to bridge the sustainable development gaps between the haves and have-nots but, more importantly, cap global warming to well below 2 degrees Celsius, I hope this chapter strengthens the case to start seeing the bigger picture of our impacts through a system thinking approach.

Reflection Pointers:

- Is there a need to approach sustainability from top-down and bottom-up initiatives? Simultaneously?
- Can leaders set the intention, believing in the best outcomes and encouraging the relevant actions required from stakeholders, especially employees and supply chains, to contribute to sustainability objectives and results?
- Does every stakeholder have a role to play in contributing to sustainability?
- How are we making sense of our own sustainability metrics?
- Is there a regular reporting mechanism in place, if not software aggregating data?
- Are our people informed on sustainability issues and behaving in appropriate ways to manage the low-carbon transition?

- How am I developing myself for sustainable leadership?
- Have we prioritised our stakeholders via mapping and understand the varying contributions we make to sustainability along our value chain?

▲

▮▮

OVERCOME POWERLESSNESS

You feel good not because the world is right, but
your world is right because you feel good.
—Wayne W. Dyer, *The Power of Intention: Learning
to Co-create Your World Your Way*

Unprecedented Change Management Required

We are in uncharted waters as we navigate the multiple transits we are taking at an individual, organisational and systems level. We know our near-term 2030 and long-term 2050 goals—nature-positive, regenerative societies and a just transition—but to make the leap may be harder for some than others. What needs to change is complex as we remain largely stuck in our sense of powerlessness to do anything different unless we are key decision-makers like governments and corporate CEOs. Nonetheless, this too has its resource and economic constraints as our financial system remains largely a monetised and capitalist one.

The resurgence of sustainability and prioritising non-financial performance is encouraging, yet the fear is that the transition might be limited by agendas of hard-to-abate industries that do not want to be outlawed or made obsolete by the sweep of a climate policy change.

How we navigate moving forward needs to be done sensitively, and the proceedings of COP27 in Dubai showed exactly this challenge in phasing out fossil fuels, something we know had to be done at previous COPs but, because of the dependence structure of our economies, is hard to change and eventually overcome. We therefore remain powerless and make small transitions instead in hopes that the lag in climate change remains under control since it manifests much later.

As Earth overshoot days draw nearer with each passing year except for when the world was under lockdown due to COVID-19, we remain powerless yet again to undo the very lifestyles and behaviours that equipped us to consume, produce, and waste more, thanks to fast-fashion, e-commerce, and cheap supply chains. As captives of our own spending habits, we remain powerless yet again to make the change needed towards sustainable living and positive change for our landfills at least.

Slowly, our governments and mobilised community groups along with some enlightened corporate coalitions push for change. Awareness is lacking. Let us raise our advocacy budget. Let us market the need to be more sustainable. But how much awareness is enough? The action gap widens.

Adjacent possibilities to create opportunities from a green transition are abundant only if we can overcome our powerless ability to see better, see beyond what is right in front of us. Green commute is important, so mass transportation services benefit from marketing this as a sustainable lifestyle shift. Thankfully, innovative start-ups, progressive policymakers are leading the way, but we need everyone to play their part. Powerlessness continues to plague us—the mountain seems too big to surmount alone. Even if I do something, it would hardly make a dent and we sit back down.

In *The Responsibility Revolution*, Jeffrey Hollender shares quick strategies: start small, stay aligned to the purpose and mission of why we want to change towards sustainability, run new efforts along with status quo operations to minimise distractions, and recruit volunteers who can be green ambassadors. Lastly, understand what worked and what did not, build the best practice, and get the decision-maker's buy-in to scale up. This might seem easier said than done.

In *Working with Presence*, Daniel Goleman has an active discourse with systems thinker Peter Senge on why we may feel powerless in these instances. So many of us get into meetings and wonder why we needed it especially if there is no space to differ and we go into a state of withdrawal. However, if we remain engaged, enquire, we can co-discover truth and insight that is greater than if we were to work within our own awareness.

Despite knowing this, we succumb to groupthink because unknowingly we feel powerlessness. Since most organisations operate as family structures, there is an implicit order to how to behave, which creates a pseudo harmony we may not want to mess with. There are hidden mental models, unspoken norms that we need to challenge but we are afraid of conflicts. Here Goleman shares that 'conflict can be productive if we know how to harness it . . . (and) bring it out productively'.[53]

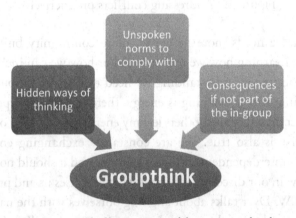

Figure 21: Challenges to tackling groupthink

---

[53]   D. Goleman and P. Senge, *Working with Presence: A Leading with Emotional Intelligence Conversation with Peter Senge*, Macmillan Audio, unabridged edition, 2006, [**audiobook**].

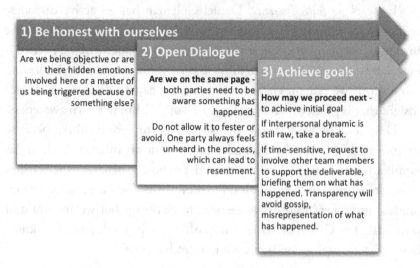

Figure 22: Addressing conflicts productively

The future needs more networks, more community building, and more of us. Learning how we feel included or how we can include others is another pertinent understanding we need to identify for ourselves. In understanding that everything is energy, there is a misconception that I must protect myself against others lest my energy gets drained or affected. The converse is also true. We are constantly exchanging energy with others. This interdependence will not go away, and it should not. Instead, we can grow in our discernment about what energises us and pursue that.

Wayne W. Dyer talks about aligning ourselves with the natural flow of intelligence that awakens our dormant forces especially when we are inspired. Sustainable leaders are therefore interconnectors. They navigate complexities of life with an all-knowing belief that we are connected in the infinite field of energy in physical and non-physical forms. Most of us get disconnected from this inner knowing, thanks to the ego that offers limiting beliefs about who and what we are. We can undo that now.

In *The Fifth Discipline*, Peter Senge promotes a 'new view of leadership', where 'leaders are designers, teachers and stewards'.[54] Most importantly, pursuing these higher ideals need not burn us out or make us think so.

---

[54]   P. Senge, *The Fifth Discipline: The Art and Practice of the Learning Organization* (revised and updated version), New York, Doubleday, 2006, p.527 **[e-book]**.

In fact, 'burnout does not come from working too hard; instead it comes from having an inaccurate view of human nature, of our own potential and limitations'.[55] When we stop over-romanticising others, we do not feel the psychological stress when they let us down.[56] To some extent, we expect it and avoid feeling hurt or disappointed eventually. However, if an organisation does not share a common mental model or vision, personal mastery will only 'increase organisational stress'.[57] This dynamic needs to be well understood. Organisations cannot promote it without adapting themselves; otherwise, it leads to counterproductivity.

Breakthroughs Required

There are six limiting beliefs described by Wayne W. Dyer in his book *Your Sacred Self.*[58]

First, *I am what I have: my possessions define me.* My personal journey in unpacking this statement begins with a chance discovery of the Netflix documentary film *Less Is Now*, talking about The Minimalists, two friends who set out to discover their meaning in life through owning less. They openly share how being raised poor and feeling this inherent lack, not having enough, made them strive for possessions that did not give them the satisfaction that they really wanted out of life. Eventually, in pursuing the philosophy of minimalism, they started taking grounded action with mindfulness. This led me to the next Netflix show—Mari Kondo and her philosophy of 'sparking joy'. In following the stories unfold in each episode as she helped clients get back on track with life, it depicts the importance of letting go and unearthing the limiting beliefs that hold us back through possessions and memories. This is when we become unbounded.

Second, *I am what I do: my achievements define me.* This was a personal truth for me until I experienced the sudden death of my father in 2017. In that moment, I grew acutely aware that no title, status of wealth, or

---

55 Senge, *The Fifth Discipline*, p. 229 [e-book].
56 Senge, *The Fifth Discipline*, p. 229.
57 Senge, *The Fifth Discipline*, p. 229.
58 W. Dyer, *Your Sacred Self: Making the Decision to Be Free*, New York, HarperCollins e-books, 2008, pp. 461-2.

grievance matters more than the lives we have touched and love rendered. In that moment, I chose to set the intention of living from my heart and not from ego, vanity, or status. It has been an uphill and rewarding journey since because people, life, and situations will always try to suck you back in. We are still a mind/identity-based society, which needs to transform into a compassion/heart-based society instead.

Third, *I am what others think of me: my reputation defines me.* When more of us realise that most people are caught up in their own activities and ego-minding, we start to be free. By the way, our ego does take up time because it needs to be constantly entertained. Also, when anyone's dark night of the soul arrives, it is 100 per cent certain we have to face it, alone. Once we realise and accept this, we unbound further and start realising our own potential. Detaching might hurt in the beginning. The ego will string a narrative: 'People do not care to check in. I am so alone/lonely. Why do people not care?' It will loop. It is up to us to move away from that by focusing on empowering thoughts: 'I am free to live the life I want, I am free to be me.' Everyone has different circumstances. This is not advocating for us to step away from responsibilities. This is about overcoming our own sense of powerlessness to achieve a more empowered state of being, anchored in self-knowledge and self-leadership to show up better as individuals at work, in our families, and in society.

Fourth, *I am separate from everyone: my body defines me as alone.* Sustainable leaders as interconnectors know that we are not separate from everything that surrounds us. They are aware that this is a form of fear that holds us back from realising our true potential. By knowing we are living in a living universe, constantly choosing and living the realities co-created by us, we have tremendous agency to see how we are also interconnected to fellow humans, plants, and animals. Sustainability is highly intersectional, which is why silo thinking needs to transform into interdisciplinary group-work because no one arena has the answers. Financial institutions know that ESG data will come from other sectors as non-financial risks grow in significance in the future.

Fifth, *I am separate from all that is missing in my life: my life space is separate from my desires.* Once we realise we are not separate, which the pandemic helped to seed in the collective consciousness, then we walk feeling supported. It is only when we believe we are not supported, we attract the related experiences. Training our subconscious mind will be continuously important. Regardless of the situation, we need to stay resilient. Knowing what we desire and believing it is possible can be an uphill task for some of us. Sustainable leaders believe it is possible and lead with stoic certainty, understanding if delays abound and if non-linear developments emerge. They ride out the waves and eventually see the shore to be the lighthouse for those they are leading.

Lastly, *I am separate from God/higher intelligence: my life depends on God's/other's assessment of my worthiness.* For most humans, judgement is instinctual. We immediately categorise or shoehorn someone based on our limited impressions and knowledge. It is simple heuristics and a legacy of our more primitive ancestors who had to ascertain if someone was a friend or foe. In today's advanced age and growth, we ought to have outgrown this instinctual habit, yet we stay captive by it. This is made worse when there are institutions involved and radical or conservative doctrine that relies on control to harness power. As such, feeling worthy as a human can be a rare commodity, and this need not be the case. We all have self-soothing and coping abilities, which we can leverage when it comes to judgement.

With our discernment abilities, we can decipher if someone's opinion is factual or subjective. Most importantly, we are wise enough to know we need to entertain all thoughts and impressions because we are in control. Sustainable leaders are zen this way. They sense make to stability with an acute desire to sieve out the noise; otherwise, it is likely one will burn out quicker than they like.

Intention to do better, let go of these limiting beliefs, cannot be accessed by the ego. We will have to bypass it and work with the subconscious and unconscious mind as shown in figure 1. Our psyches are wired uniquely. Working with a trusted accountability partner can help show you what is being projected, what mirrors around you are sending back as feedback, and most importantly, help you figure out where your destination point is.

Dyer offers four strategies to transcend:

1. **Discipline**: training our mind to activate intentions/desires to deactivate ego identification, toxic patterns and learn healthier habits

2. **Wisdom**: staying focused and being patient as we harmonise our feelings, thoughts, and intellect

3. **Love**: loving what we do and doing what we love—from enjoying the feeling, to sharing what we love with others, to continuously practising and developing ourselves

4. **Surrender**: this is the stage where the body and mind are no longer running the show, and grace emerges to guide us. We lighten up and are in touch with our infinite selves, and natural intelligence to receive guidance to achieve our desires.

Once we master this, we can no longer keep people at the periphery because they become less invested in 'we are all the same here'. Sustainable leaders and teams alike can benefit from presencing. This is the act of 'really hearing what the other is saying to feel it next and then walk in each other's shoes to sense the situation at the deepest level, which is what is the purpose that brings us together'.[59] Leaders who practise this have the ability to pay attention, articulate vision/mission, and set priorities that resonate with people. They also step back to see freshly since we do need to suspend ourselves to see our hidden thinking models that include assumptions, biases, and cognitive distortions.

Learning is highly personalised and varies from group to group because of differing context, culture, technology, etc. There is no fixed formula, but certain tools and principles, such as encouraging aspiration, conversation, understanding complexity, and practising these tools, help.[60]

Regaining power to engage and contribute to organisations hence requires the capacity to suspend assumptions, develop purposefulness, engage in dialogue and systems thinking, and encourage organisational learning. High-performance teams achieve this with how they respond, and this prolongs the viability of the organisation in the long term. We need to enable such teams instead of allowing powerlessness to set in and disintegrate our every attempt and progress to be sustainable financially and more.

---

[59] D. Goleman and P. Senge, *Working with Presence: A Leading with Emotional Intelligence Conversation with Peter Senge*, location, Macmillan Audio, unabridged edition, 2006 [**audiobook**].

[60] Goleman and Senge, *Working with Presence*.

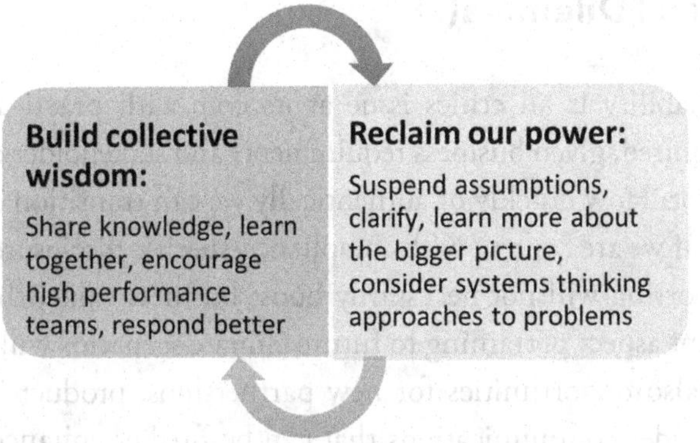

Build collective wisdom:

Share knowledge, learn together, encourage high performance teams, respond better

Reclaim our power:

Suspend assumptions, clarify, learn more about the bigger picture, consider systems thinking approaches to problems

Figure 23: When we are self-empowered,
we can strengthen communities

Leveraging our top talents to master and then, as a group, be more aware of what is really needed and do what is next is collectively attuning. When our brains harmonise to a collective flow state rather than focus on personal intelligence, our organisations run well. Much of learning is tacit to tacit, with the importance of stories and how they get transferred.[61] This begins with diminishing the us-them divide and improving our quality of being, which comes from being more connected within ourselves and each other.

In sum, powerlessness needs to be addressed by substituting effort with intelligence, collective intelligence. We need to focus on key issues, instead of working harder. Like for waste management—do we start collecting more waste streams or encourage more recycling or encourage less consumption upstream? With collective intelligence applied to learn and respond, the level of awareness and confidence from mutual empathy will reduce waste efficiently because we can understand the depth of the issue and how we contribute to it, in many ways.

---

[61]   D. Goleman and P. Senge, *Working with Presence: A Leading with Emotional Intelligence Conversation with Peter Senge,* Macmillan Audio, unabridged edition, 2006 [**audiobook**].

The Ethical Dilemma(s)

Sustainability is an ethics issue at its core with practical decision-making required, given business requirements and stakeholder expectation management. How quickly or authentically we can transition depends on leadership. If we are content with compliance-specific disclosure and know further reporting will not necessarily boost business value, then the risk management aspect pertaining to future climate scenarios will be missed. There are also opportunities for new partnerships, product innovation, and stakeholder communications that can be further enhanced through a reporting cycle. As such, this is why we need to do the productive thing instead of the bare minimum.

However, the solution for sustainability is a multi-stakeholder one, requiring frontline to enterprise risk managers to supply-chain business partners to engage together since everyone has a different piece of the business puzzle. The main challenge is ensuring we all see and perceive social and environmental impacts by the company or faced by the company as the same. Furthermore, environment, social, and governance (ESG) or climate reporting has been largely voluntary till recently with regulators stepping up mandatory disclosures. There is still no official policing body to govern the disclosures, whether independently validated or not, as factual. Even if so, the next step would be to correspond with relevant spatial data to cross-check and verify, preferably with stakeholder feedback pertaining to a business unit or location.

Most organisations are worried about the workload that comes with conceptualising a reporting framework to procuring more complete datasets and disclosing them as accurately as possible. This has its own issues, given the frameworks and standards for sustainability reporting are time-consuming as it involves different reporting streams to consolidate at one point. This is why certain regulators are developing their own taxonomy and means to make sense of these disclosures instead.[62]

---

[62]   L. Rhick, *No one left behind: Simplified guide hopes to push sustainability disclosures among Malaysian SMEs*, Eco-Business, https://www.eco-business.com/news/no-one-left-behind-simplified-guide-hopes-to-push-sustainability-disclosures-among-malaysian-smes/ (accessed 26 January 2024).

However, data accuracy and relevance of reporting is where the emphasis needs to be, even if data is third-party verified. Most of us are reporting for the sake of, when there ought to be a corresponding system to validate our claims and let us know our remaining carbon/social capital budget.

In a way, the Science-Based Targets Initiative (SBTI) does this as its process, which has its limitations as it treats each reporting entity as unique when we need a networked system that can communicate with each other seamlessly and cross-check. In a way, the ESG ranking systems do this on behalf of investors, but with each entity honing its own proprietary methodology, the nuances of ESG focus vary along with depth, given the intersectionality nature of sustainability, cutting across many different verticals.

This is upending the typical silo culture that most organisations operate in the name of operational efficiency and good governance. We portion off bits of the business to different business units, and while they excel at what they do, sustainability is asking for business units to speak to each other and create new value instead. Teething issues will be natural as we overcome the territorial tendencies of human nature while managing sensitive boundaries to ensure balance and harmony can be achieved. This in principle is the hardest part of getting to net zero. Once we win people, the rest is doable.

Climate Debt Challenge

'Climate debt can be estimated based on actual and projected emissions and the social cost of carbon, which measures the economic damage per ton of CO_2 emissions.'[63] The International Monetary Fund (IMF) reports our 'climate debt to be extremely large—some $59 trillion over the period of 1959 to 2018, projected to increase by another $80 trillion during 2019 to 2035'.[64]

---

[63]   B. Clements; S. Gupta; J. Liu, 'Settling the Climate Debt', *Finance and Development*, p. 54, https://www.imf.org/en/Publications/fandd/issues/2023/09/settling-the-climate-debt-clements-gupta-liu (accessed 26 January 2024).

[64]   Clements et al, 'Settling the Climate Debt', p.54.

In 2011, Bangkok experienced record-breaking rains which caused the Chao Phraya River to flood with an estimated twelve billion tons of water, killing more than 800 people and damaging infrastructure across seven industrial parks, affecting 730 companies, in the northern suburbs.[65] Although a similar flood recurring has been described to have a 1 per cent chance in any given year, future-proofing our businesses remain pivotal as rising temperatures are bringing on higher incidences of natural disasters and related health and sourcing risks for materials and resources including manpower.[66]

Today, we are experiencing a higher frequency of physical risks resulting from extreme weather patterns such as floods and wildfires, which has a financial impact on business operations and eventual sustainability of the brand, its product or service. According to Aon's 2023 Weather, Climate, and Catastrophe Report: 'Natural disasters caused global economic losses of about $313 billion in 2022 (and) less than half of this among was insured'.[67] This affects our resilience quotient especially if our suppliers or customers are found in vulnerable locations.

Stopping plastic production to tackle plastic waste is another global conundrum. With negotiations ongoing in 2023 till an internationally binding global plastics treaty is in force end of 2024, virgin plastic made from chemicals sourced from fossil fuel is only expected to increase, which environmental groups argue needs to stop.[68] Equally, scientists

[65] Nikkei Asia, *Global companies must learn from Thai floods that upended supply chains*, 13 October 2021, https://asia.nikkei.com/Opinion/The-Nikkei-View/ Global-companies-must-learn-from-Thai-floods-that-upended-supply-chains (accessed 26 January 2024).

[66] Nikkei Asia, *Global companies must learn from Thai floods that upended supply chains*; FTSE Russell, *The COP28 Net Zero Atlas*, November 2023, https://www. lseg.com/content/dam/ftse-russell/en_us/documents/research/cop28-net-zero-atlas.pdf (accessed 26 January 2024).

[67] Boston Consulting Group, How Insurers Can Innovate in Response to Extreme Weather Events, 10 October 2023, https://www.bcg.com/publications/2023/ how-insurers-can-innovate-in-response-to-extreme-weather-events (accessed 26 January 2024).

[68] M. Copley, *Global talks to cut plastic waste stall as industry and environmental groups clash*, NPR, https://www.npr.org/2023/11/20/1214141053/un-plastic-waste-pollution-negotiations-treaty-kenya-fossil-fuel-climate-change (accessed 26 January 2024).

are pushing for legally binding targets to reduce plastics production.[69] Oil and gas lobbyists on the other hand are promoting recycling, proper waste management, and keeping waste out of the environment to continue producing new plastics to avoid sunsetting their industry.[70] The plastic overshoot day, which was projected to occur on 28 July 2023, is the day plastic waste generated exceeds our ability to manage waste, leading to environmental pollution, including the marine environment.[71]

Given the competing nature of business-as-usual and climate transition plans, individual approaches to ethical management of sustainability disclosures are either unknowingly disregarded, left to a few individuals in middle management, or outsourced to consultants even if the legal liability of reporting falls on top and senior management as part of good corporate governance.

This has been largely due to the voluntary nature of sustainability reporting and therefore business prioritisation, which then requires a rethink about what a successful business model is in this age and time. As regulators move towards mandatory regulations, moving beyond disclosures towards accurate verification of reporting needs to be considered. As climate litigation cases rise, it is good that the judiciary is getting equipped with the critical knowledge required to assess climate claims legitimacy.[72]

---

[69] N. Jones, *Progress on plastic pollution treaty too slow, scientists say*, Nature, 20 November 2023, https://www.nature.com/articles/d41586-023-03579-1 (accessed 26 January 2024); The Scientists' Coalition for an Effective Plastics Treaty, a group of some 250 experts from about fifty nations, is pushing for an agreement that will set legally binding targets to reduce plastics production, both for each signing party and for the planet as a whole.

[70] M. Copley, *Global talks to cut plastic waste stall as industry and environmental groups clash*, NPR, https://www.npr.org/2023/11/20/1214141053/un-plastic-waste-pollution-negotiations-treaty-kenya-fossil-fuel-climate-change (accessed 26 January 2024).

[71] S. Perreard, et al, *Plastic Overshoot Day*, https://plasticovershoot.earth/wp-content/uploads/2023/06/EA_POD_report_2023-V3.pdf, Environmental Action, p. 14 (accessed 26 January 2024).

[72] D. Fogarty, *See you in court: training equips Asian judges for climate litigation cases*, The Straits Times, 15 Nov 2023, https://www.straitstimes.com/asia/see-you-in-court-training-equips-asian-judges-for-climate-litigation-cases (accessed 26 January 2024).

A big word has overshadowed what little climate ambition a company may have had: net zero. This buzzword has also allowed many leading companies to argue that achieving it would require herculean efforts and data as well as technology that is yet to be available or market-ready. On the other hand, investment firms have sourced emerging breakthrough research and development and are expediting the commercialisation and scaling of applications. Yes, getting to net zero is challenging, and we can all be a part of the solution—let us stretch our mental models.

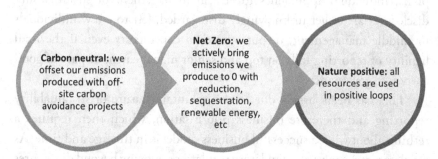

Figure 24: Progressive steps for large existing systems to be nature positive although this is non-linear and non-causation. One can leap directly to nature positive if designing new assets/products/services.

Green Corruption?

The Basel Institute of Governance reports that on a global scale, an estimated USD100 billion could be saved annually if climate-related corruption risks were addressed. This is the equivalent of the amount needed for developing countries via the loss and damages fund. But the world lacks data because there is no framework for collecting data on climate finance or corruption.[73]

The Basel Institute of Governance 'works with global public and private sectors and civil society to bring a follow-the-money approach

---

[73] D. Fogarty, *See you in court: training equips Asian judges for climate litigation cases,* The Straits Times, 15 Nov 2023, https://www.straitstimes.com/asia/see-you-in-court-training-equips-asian-judges-for-climate-litigation-cases (accessed 26 January 2024).

to the fight against illegal wildlife trade (IWT), forest crimes, illegal mining, and other environmental crimes. This includes supporting our law enforcement partners to build investigative capacity to trace illicit funds and confiscate the proceeds of crime. The aim is to make it much more difficult to profit from environmental crime for criminal organisations, unscrupulous corporations and corrupt officials that are exploiting our planet for personal gain'.[74]

Corruption is a systemic risk that has prevailed across time and has clear negative impacts on climate mitigation.[75] Because of corruption, less is available to invest in climate management projects, which reduces the efficacy of governments, with the possibility of diluting climate policies and political will should conflict of interests or lobbying occur.[76] More than 75 per cent of climate funds raised are expensed in the same countries that funded them when more vulnerable regions like Africa receive less than 5.5 per cent for contributing less than 8 per cent of global greenhouse gases.[77] By 2030, we will require an estimated $4.5 trillion annually, raised to $6 trillion yearly by 2050.[78]

According to Transparency International, corruption has been the main reason why global peace has been undermined for the past fifteen years by weak trust in governance institutions and conflicts generating more opportunities for corruption.[79] By increasing transparency of

---

[74]   Basel Institute on Governance, *Green Corruption*, 2024, https://baselgovernance. org/green-corruption (accessed 26 January 2024).

[75]   Transparency International, *The Impact of Corruption on the Climate is Profound*, https://www.transparency.org/en/projects/climate-governance-integrity-programme/climate-corruption-atlas (accessed 26 January 2024).

[76]   A. Cabrejo le Roux *Is the Climate Crisis a Corruption Crisis? An Interview with Brice Bohmer,* Basel Institute on Governance, 30 August 2023, https:// baselgovernance.org/news/climate-crisis-corruption-crisis-interview-brice-bohmer (accessed 26 January 2024).

[77]   R. Al-Mashat, *Climate financing that puts people first,* International Monetary Fund: Finance and Development, September 2023, https://www.imf.org/en/Publications/fandd/issues/2023/09/POV-climate-financing-that-puts-people-first-rania-al-mashat (accessed 26 January 2024).

[78]   Al-Mashat, *Climate financing that puts people first.*

[79]   Transparency International, *Corruption Perceptions Index,* https://www.transparency.org/en/cpi/2022 (accessed 26 January 2024).

decision-making by providing public engagement and democratic platforms, corruption can be weeded out to achieve eventual peace.[80]

Co-Investment Required for Just Transition

In 2023, *Forbes* reported that human ingenuity has already led to energy-efficiency-related innovations like sustainable aviation fuel, carbon capture technologies, and automation solutions, along with increased public-private partnerships.[81] In Singapore, the successful completion of a twenty-month pilot of sustainable aviation fuel (SAF) initiated in February 2022 shows that the republic is operationally ready to supply SAF, albeit more support is needed to increase adoption, because of financial constraints.[82] With the generation of SAF credits in partnership with local carbon exchanges such as Climate Impact X, corporates will be able to offset their travel emissions and generate additional financing to compensate for the high cost in adopting SAF for now.[83]

However, according to the UN, 'developing countries have borne the brunt (over 95 per cent) of credit rating downgrades, despite experiencing relatively milder economic contractions'.[84] This impacts the countries' cost of borrowing and the financial market stability.[85] There is a need to

---

[80] Transparency International, *Corruption Perceptions Index*.

[81] G. Towler, *Human Ingenuity Is Key To Climate Action*, Forbes, https://www.forbes.com/sites/honeywell/2023/11/27/human-ingenuity-is-key-to-climate-action/?sh=59f829c19c38 (accessed 26 January 2024).

[82] Civil Aviation Authority of Singapore (CAAS), *Singapore Is Operationally Ready for Sustainable Aviation Fuel But More Is Needed to Support Adoption*, https://www.caas.gov.sg/who-we-are/newsroom/Detail/singapore-is-operationally-ready-for-sustainable-aviation-fuel-but-more-is-needed-to-support-adoption (accessed 26 January 2024).

[83] CAAS, *Singapore is Operationally Ready for Sustainable Aviation Fuel But More is Needed to Support Adoption*.

[84] UN Department of Economic and Social Affairs, *Policy Brief No. 131: Credit Rating Agencies and Sovereign Debt: Four proposals to support achievement of the SDGs*, United Nations, https://www.un.org/development/desa/dpad/wp-content/uploads/sites/45/publication/PB_131_final.pdf (accessed 26 January 2024).

[85] UN, *Policy Brief No. 131*.

incorporate 'climate change and other non-economic factors into rating methodologies'.[86]

As we consider restructuring the global financial architecture to accelerate blended finance, via the Bridgetown Initiative and the G20 Capital Adequacy Framework, for example, what would be a common platform or messaging for all of us to get on board look like? How can we convince ourselves that a just transition premised on equitable allocation of benefits and burdens is inclusive, necessary, and important for all of us, not just those of us who may feel compelled or the marginalised seeking reparations.

IMF's former president Minouche Shafik in her book *What We Owe Each Other: A New Social Contract for a Better Society* shares deep insights on how we need a social contract built on better architecture to provide security for all with efficient and fair sharing of risks, along with opportunities that invest in capabilities. These are not new concepts. She references John F. Kennedy's 'declaration of interdependence' from 1962, which mentions 'mutually beneficial gains to be had from cooperation'. In 1967, Martin Luther King talked about the 'inescapable network of mutuality'.

Currently, our demographic and technological changes are creating we-are-on-our-own societies. This according to Shafik is inequitable, to depend on individuals, and far less efficient and productive than sharing across society.[87]

How we operate internationally and strengthen depends on whether our national social contract is just. The architecture of opportunity needs to fair to be more generous towards others. The social protection floor initiative of the International Labour Organisation (ILO) aims at this objective, with 'higher productivity as an aim' by 'tapping into all capabilities in society to include untapped talent, raise innovation potential, and reduce the need

[86]   UN, *Policy Brief No. 131.*

[87]   S. Minouche, *What We Owe Each Other: A New Social Contract for a Better Society,* New Jersey, Princeton University Press, 2021, pp. 68, 235-6, 301-2, 332, 373-4 **[e-book]**.

to redistribute income'.[88] With fairer division of labour, especially care workers, labour markets need to be both flexible and secure.[89]

David Kantor, an American systems psychologist and pioneer in systems-centred therapy, posits that once we begin to understand and change how we are interdependent within our family or organisational structures, we 'free people from previously mysterious forces that dictated their behaviour'.[90] This is how we may all overcome our powerlessness, by building coalitions that restore our environment, creating new possibilities, providing regenerative and effective product solutions, inspiring conscious consumption, and most importantly, creating a just and equitable world.[91]

These changes will require deeper transformations to encourage greater transparency and ease. In *Theory U*, C. Otto Scharmer provides the presencing grammar for us to navigate this space. It might seem like these values are difficult to attain, and that is because we lack an understanding of what causes social systems to behave the way they do.

Aristotle, ancient Greek philosopher and scientist, has provided us this clarity with his four causes: (1) material cause, (2) formal cause, (3) final cause, and (4) efficient cause stemming from agency or beginning of movement. Material cause relates to how a structure is determined, while formal cause relates to its respective functions. Final cause determines the explanation for the function, its purpose, while efficient cause relates to our behaviours. These aspects combine provide a holistic overview of our challenges and opportunities to progress within our social systems and achieve 'self-determination or freedom' according to Scharmer.[92]

The ideal freedom state would be developing a 'resilience capability derived from a sustainable business model activated through relationships among internal and external stakeholders and supported by an ethical-based transformational leadership model which, in turn, derives from and

---

88   Minouche, *What We Owe Each Other*, Chapter 5: Work.

89   Minouche, *What We Owe Each Other*, Chapter 5: Work.

90   P. Senge, *The Fifth Discipline: The Art and Practice of the Learning Organization* (revised and updated version), New York, Doubleday, 2006, p.368 [**e-book**].

91   J. Hollender and B.Breen *The Responsibility Revolution: How the Next Generation of Businesses Will Win*, San Francisco, Jossey-Bass, 2010, p.30 [**e-book**].

92   Refer to figure 20.1: Four Causes, Four Types of Causation. O. Scharmer *Theory U: Leading from the Future as It Emerges*, California, Berrett-Koehler Publishers, 2009, pp. 878-9 [**e-book**].

nurtures the coherence among the mission-governance and accountability model'.[93] Value would be intended as 'sustainable value, expressed in terms of economic, social, ethical environmental performances'.[94]

We will need new vocabulary for this, which is thankfully emerging. We will need to take action over rhetoric or mere setting intentions and exercise the logic of reciprocity over gratuity.[95] We will also need to widen the measurements of our business impact. For instance, with regards to carbon emission reductions, owning authoritative and neutral data in terms of carbon, cost and time, and where possible, an internal carbon price, can help us take action on carbon abatement projects and encourage our value chain to echo the same savings in their initiatives.

In the words of Jonathan Labrey, albeit from 2015 but still relevant: 'The world needs a comprehensive reassessment of our understanding of value—its parameters and its effects—to restore trust in economic and business decision-making and achieve investment that contributes towards financial stability and sustainable development. We must ensure that business models sing to the tune of a value creation model fit for the twenty-first century'.[96]

Reflection Pointers:

- Do I agree I have the power to make some changes in my personal or professional life towards a better life for all?
- For existing business models that want to pivot to a sustainable business model, please evaluate your reason for being from a people and planet perspective.

---

[93] D. Baldo and M.G. Baldarelli, 'Renewing and improving the business model toward sustainability in theory and practice', Int J Corporate Soc Responsibility 2, 3, 2017, p. 2, https://doi.org/10.1186/s40991-017-0014-z

[94] D. Baldo and M.G. Baldarelli, 'Renewing and improving the business model toward sustainability in theory and practice', p.2.

[95] D. Baldo and M.G. Baldarelli, 'Renewing and improving the business model toward sustainability in theory and practice', p.8.

[96] L. Jonathan, Chief Strategy Office, International Integrated Reporting Council-IIRC, Paris, 6 May 2015.

- How is the business having a net positive impact on the environment?
- Does this include broader considerations of biodiversity, ecosystem services both upstream and downstream?
- What is the minimal environmental scope the business can focus to assure customers it is working on improving its sustainability footprint?
- How is the business actively serving the society in which it operates?
- Who are some target stakeholders the company could work with, such as youth or elderly? Best if this complements the business objectives of growing brand awareness within the consumer group within your niche business field.
- Does the business give back to its stakeholders who contributed to its success?

III

OWN WHAT WE CAN KNOW

Unlocking Institutional Knowledge

There are limits to knowledge—either we do not have the time, bandwidth to know everything we need to know or there are aptitude and attitudinal challenges. We may not be interested to begin with.

These inherent blocks aside, the logistical challenge with knowing what we can know is, first, where is information stored? Who are the main personnel to approach? Why is the information stored this way and how may we consolidate and democratise access in an easy-to-search manner for all to be aware at any point of time? This is especially as we operate increasingly in clouds and have ready access to information on the Web.

Some of us who like to be more responsible over our particular work streams may be uncomfortable with the notion of open access and transparency, especially if there are team members who are able to market themselves better and give a certain impression to leaders that work was managed by them. It is here where a well-designed system would provide traceability of ownership for all leaders to assess and verify accordingly.

Capitalising on institutional knowledge shared across the generations of employees can also help identify the loopholes, inefficiencies, and opportunities to do better in mitigating operational risks pertaining to sustainability or physical/transition risks. This is an uphill and challenging task for small and more technologically advanced organisations alike.

Where should we begin? How far back in history is useful for a trends analysis especially as near-term conditions continuously evolve, creating chaotic conditions for decisive action. It is no wonder most of us cling to business-as-usual because of the complexity. However, from a societal standpoint, we need to start this consolidation at some point.

As organisations, specifically listed companies, report on various ESG metrics such as carbon, energy, waste, water, and various occupational health and safety (OHS), social, and governance metrics, the need to consider their overall impact score on business and community resilience is helpful from both the business and the people and planet standpoint.

In chaos engineering, a position within the system greatly impacts one's ability to change it. By understanding the current system and the level of institutional knowledge available, we can monitor the outcome and then define a variable that we plan to intentionally change in order to further monitor the outcome, and any related new, emergent behaviour to compare system performance to its previous state of being. This creates effective feedback loops within the experiment, which is at the core of how we create successful change within the organisation.[97]

As difficult as it sounds, paving new communication channels to avoid pitfalls of communication breakdown while maintaining speed and effectiveness will be necessary.[98] For businesses, this would be limiting the number of people relationships to somewhere around 150 to hold and maintain stable relationships with. Team members are encouraged to create connections and relationships with folks on different teams, to expand their networks since many of the challenges we deal with in distributed systems can be mapped to challenges within an organisation.

At some point, ownership and accountability ultimately end up on the shoulders of the system's leader. Here decisions are made within a bounded context—the leader becomes accountable for the choice made. Local rationality, described as what makes sense from one person's perspective,

---

[97]   C. Rosenthal and N. Jones, *Chaos Engineering: System Resiliency in Practice*, California, O'Reilly Media, 2020, p. 296, [**e-book**].

[98]   Rosenthal and Jones, *Chaos Engineering*, p. 306.

may not make sense from someone else's. We will therefore have to focus on creating a non-threatening culture where different perspectives are acceptable, according to sociologist Ron Westrum. In order for system or organisational safety to improve, it is increasingly important to evaluate what we do well and learn to do less, better. Tools do not create resilience; they help people create resilience.[99]

All of this, however, will require a certain attitude of wanting to improve productivity. Many of us are content with status quo, unaware of what needs to change and uncomfortable with rocking any boat, especially if it comes with more work, a certain backlash or consequence. It is here where the leader needs to be discerning with the team to play out the pros and cons of ideas and brainstorm how well it integrates into their quarterly, half-yearly, yearly, or longer work plans.

A knowledge management system inbuilt with a learning management system to onboard new staff or stakeholders to the business operations is beneficial as organisations grow more complex. A one-stop hub, virtual information sharing together with peer-to-peer mentoring can boost both motivations to learn and grow the company's knowledge assets, in order to pivot timely and source new innovations. This requires an open culture, one that is preferably generative and rewards new ideas and perspectives. Leaders are welcoming to change and encourage consistent optimisation to how work is done to achieve productivity gains.

Allowing Information Sharing

Information is power and everyone deserves it. Most times, we do a bad job in storing it and then forget to recall it—wasting further time and effort, and reinventing many wheels that were previously already in motion. When we lose this superpower, we lose out on productivity hours, something for leaders to mull over.

Information flow is deeply linked to establishing an inclusive, engaged, and participative culture as organisations get more mission-oriented

---

[99] Rosenthal and Jones, *Chaos Engineering*, p. 259 [e-book].

and less personal.[100] This requires establishing types of activities that are acceptable. Better information just leads to better organisations since organisations function on information. How well information flows reflects on its culture. When people trust one another, information flows, but when there is no trust, it becomes a political commodity.

Based on Westrum's typology, generative environments are more likely to provide information with these characteristics since they encourage a level playing field and respect for the needs of the information recipient versus pathological environments caused by leader's desire to see themselves succeed, which often create a political environment for information that interferes with good flow.[101]

Openness and transparency are both integral parts of information flow. Further, other important features of good information flow include relevance, timeliness, and clarity.[102]

Information flow brings together culture and management style.[103] When understanding why information about anomalies does not flow to people who need it, it is because individuals often remain ignorant, unaware of their own biases that interfered with search and with information flow. They also think they are critical in the information flow but get left out. Additionally, pluralistic ignorance heightens our sense of powerlessness due to an implicit reluctance to report something no one else seems to be reporting.

Building a healthy culture is hence crucial, especially in how we accept and process information. For generative cultures where there is high flow of information, certain conditions exist. There is 'high cooperation, emphasis on the mission, boundary-less organisation, psychological safety, and high

---

[100] R. Westrum, 'The study of information flow: a personal journey', *Elsevier Safety Science,* August 2014, https://www.researchgate.net/publication/261186680_ The_study_of_information_flow_A_personal_journey (accessed 26 January 2024).

[101] R. Westrum 'A typology of organisational cultures', article, *Quality and Safety in Health Care,* Research Gate Publications, January 2005, https://www. researchgate.net/publication/8150380 (accessed 26 January 2024).

[102] Westrum, 'A typology of organisational cultures', p. ii23.

[103] Westrum, 'A typology of organisational cultures', p. ii27.

creativity'.[104] Westrum exemplifies this with *Star Trek*, where we can see the high-trust and low-blame culture in play. This culture tends to support high-performance leaders who are able to grasp key questions and details, have high standards and a hands-on-attitude.[105]

This healthy culture tends to be more profitable, given the quality and flow of information and responses to failures in the system are supported with conscious inquiry as an attempt to get to the root causes of the problem and the decision-useful kind of timely information that meets the receivers' needs.[106] Here, psychological safety is pivotal, and if not existent, a change in leadership could make these changes happen.[107]

Recognising Intergenerational Impact

I make a solo trip to the Dachau Concentration Camp with a tour group. I am thankful it is summer as we walk around on the grounds. My colleague who went in winter shared how miserable and difficult it was to walk about, not to mention all the prisoners only had one layer of clothing on, with not much muscle mass to help cope with the bitter temperatures.

My tour guide is clearly passionate or working hard for his tips. He brings us to every nook and cranny of this sprawling facility. He has just finished telling us about the gas chambers and instructed those who wanted to enter to reconvene in a few minutes. I stand arrested at my spot. My heart does not let me enter, and neither does my imagination allow me to picture the experiences in that space. I stand solemnly, almost as if I was saying a quiet prayer for history not to repeat itself. And yet it does, time and time again. My thoughts are disrupted with a friendly question from the guide.

In another time, I am in Nuremberg, listening to the video testimonies of the war trial proceedings, while peering into the very hall where the sessions took place. There is something highly clinical and sanitised about

104   R. Westrum 'A typology of organisational cultures', article, *Quality and Safety in Health Care*, Research Gate Publications, January 2005, p. ii23, https://www.researchgate.net/publication/8150380 (accessed 26 January 2024).
105   Westrum, 'A typology of organisational cultures', p. ii23.
106   Westrum, 'A typology of organisational cultures', p. ii25.
107   Westrum, 'A typology of organisational cultures', p. ii26.

this space. I appreciate the modernist interior with many visual and sound aids to understand bits and pieces of the history being re-enacted from a time most of us would rather not relive, yet here it is played daily as a reminder that it happened.

In another time, juxtaposed against the gothic city of Erfurt, I walk silently past the cells conserved at the DDR Museum. My friends from Myanmar are intently listening to the tour guide. Back home, political prisoners becoming politicians was common, especially under Nobel Peace Prize laureate Aung San Suu Kyi's leadership. They comment that at least this cell is sanitary. There is a short laugh as we return to listening to the English translations of our guide through our headsets.

In another time, I stand outside the Tuol Sleng Genocide Museum. I had visited it as a backpacker in my undergraduate days and now I was back years later with my stakeholders. The atmosphere unfortunately unchanged—almost welcoming outside until you enter to witness history at a standstill with actual torture items and experiences retold. I wait outside for the group to return. After some time, we noticed familiar faces, no longer smiling but rather solemn. I share a comforting look with my Sri Lankan stakeholder. Cheerfully, I announce, 'Shopping, anyone? We will be heading to the Russian Market next.'

Each time I watch a historical biopic or an autobiographical movie, it becomes increasingly clear that many of our current struggles are universal across time and space. And if so, then why is it that we continue to experience these pains and largely disharmonious living within and with ourselves? This is of course a rhetorical and existential question. The truth is, we prefer to be numbed out with various distractions and evasion of anything potentially stir-worthy to live in an illusion that we find comfortable with.

And this I recall realising when I caught a Singapore theatre production. The story unfolds in a rich household with an engagement to be announced. However, an officer intrudes quite abruptly, and the rest of the play is plagued with uncovering who murdered an ex-lover. Over the course of an hour, a seemingly put-together household falls apart as secrets and shadow sides reveal themselves with an eventual confession to the crime by one of the family members, only for the play to end with another officer showing up for questioning. The first officer was probably a ghost or a mirage of their collective conscience—the play ended abruptly after. But an illusion was clearly formed to which the characters purged their innermost selves, both awakening and ending much of the facade of living they had managed to uphold till then.

Intergenerationally, our ancestors experienced and processed related trauma in conflict or emergency situations, even when migrating to 'better lands'. It is not surprising that we still have this behaviour set internalised within us, projecting these fears knowingly, unknowingly, thinking they are ours when in reality they belong to someone else (read more in Mark Wolynn's book *It Did Not Start with You*).

Yet most organisations as well have to deal with the legacies and impacts of intergenerational co-working dynamics. Whilst cultural expectations of how work can be done have evolved towards the less formal and more technologically advanced, the methods and expectations of older colleagues remain stuck in their times, creating space for deadlock rather than dialogue. Similarly, the unwillingness of younger colleagues to discuss why certain best practices in one colleague's opinion are not necessarily their perspective can be infuriating. We turn up with our walls up, with little to no provision to understand where the other is coming from, causing much disharmony that is common at workplaces if left to fester. There is no right cultural fix; it is just a matter of opening dialogue spaces for perspectives to be shared, and this is important for differences in approaches to be understood and a common ground to be found.

Change Is A Constant

It sounds nerve-racking to witness, perhaps—most people do not want to fall apart. We hold on so tightly sometimes even when it starts to hurt us back, but we refuse to let go because we are afraid where the tsunami of a tide will take us. As audience members, we notice the gradual release of burdens each character unknowingly, knowingly carried as the play slowly concluded. To me, this is good. Having personally gone through this myself, if done in a safe and supportive environment, each one of us would be closer to reaching our true potential.

We all want to feel certain, be assured, and have control over our lives. I pause as I write this sentence because this is such a big reason why I have struggled, strived, overachieved. Thinking we are not enough or another is not enough for us is happening only within us. External conditions may trigger these insecure feelings, but it is primarily occurring within us, if we stay still enough to hear them.

There is also a tendency to want things instantly and expect everything to go as we wish for it to, until a crisis hits, be it personal or professional, individual, or collective. At first there is denial or a certain sense of numbness and even apathy to the extent of discomfort it brings to us. We ignore it, thinking that we do not have to deal with it now or it does not affect us. However, we fail to notice the niggling feeling that builds within us, until it grows into a gnawing sense of dread living in general. We start over-consuming, losing consciousness of our surroundings and, most times, ourselves.

The likelihood of this impacting others is also high as we show up clouded in our own dark thoughts. Some of us can mask and give off appearances that externally we appear intact when internally the termites are well settled—apologies for the graphic imagery. When the realisation hits that it's termites, some of us are deep in the abyss of poor mental health or undergoing an illness or walking away from unhealthy relationships. This is non-exhaustive.

When we disconnect from ourselves, we unfortunately start to see everything as separate from us. A sense of loneliness creeps in, and soon we find ourselves lonely even in a group of people! How uncanny. Now the only solution is that we start going home to ourselves as soon as possible, but for most of us, this scares us, even more so depending on which generations we represent and how we are expected to perform in society.

We start to see it as a death wish to isolate ourselves from the very things we wish to regain connection with again, life. But it is in the self-isolation or mindful practice of being with ourselves for those brief moments, hours, or days that we start to quieten our very busy minds. Slowly and surely, we get better at it and start to see clearer. That is it: clarity in seeing, knowing, being. So those of us who have had to undergo quarantines or isolation have had the privilege of undergoing vipassana retreats in disguise—a detox of our minds. As we grow 'crazy' with this illusion of being alone, we soon realise with each passing day that a day has passed and we survived. We are independent of attachments from before. We are free agents.

Ideally, this self-isolation practice grows into a daily practice of loving ourselves and acknowledging that we as a human system, matter. That 'I am' presence is our first step towards feeling less separated/divided within ourselves.

When we connect with ourselves, we call all our senses home. We never feel lonely because we are filling every moment with our awareness. There is no time to think about anything else. When we crave, we come from a place of lack when the reality is we lack nothing. Our environments may appear to limit us, but as Dr Wayne Dyer teaches, circumstances reveal us to ourselves. For that, we should be thankful, and we are, in no way or form, limited, only if we become our own limits, which is usually the case. We internalise external beliefs or projections of what others think about us when we inherently know who we are but feel burdened to act a certain way to keep up appearances, maintain 'harmony' while we, well, live in disharmony with ourselves until it shows us. For some sooner than others, for some when we feel safe to let go, for some when we can no longer bear to hurt ourselves anymore—which was my case.

We all know the benefits of meditative awareness, the practice of non-judgement, and gratitude are plenty. But practising them takes discipline! But when we do, we start to notice the sight, smell, sound, taste again in a different way from before. Food starts to taste different because we are no longer chomping them down in some rush or guilt. We acknowledge the ground we stand on and the power of being in this space right now and how us existing in this space right now is the only thing that *truly* matters. We let go of needing to control others because we recognise one another's spirit. We recognise ourselves in the other. This in fact is the true victory of our era. When we gain this insight, we achieve this innate freedom and, in the process, set others free as well.

From this space of being, we can build up to anything, anyone. We can be invincible. We are not separate. We are always connected, to each other, to the elements, to all the universe and its constellations. We are also meant to be unique, each with our own gifts and talents, even if we fail to see it ourselves. Each one of us is important to someone, including strangers. We impact others daily in our interactions. At some point, all of us are called to address the suppressed sides to us so that we can return to wholeness. It is during this time that we ask ourselves: *How can we accept ourselves authentically, as we are?*

Putting limits on ourselves closes us up to the wonders of our universe that is multifaceted and creative at the source of it all. Allowing ourselves to just be taps into the pure potentiality of our existence and propels us forward on a path beyond our own imaginings. If we do not resist, that is. So often we do, out of fear or some compulsion to hold on to baggage or pain because it is more familiar than what is waiting for us on the other side: pure creative potential. It is understandably scary like how the path less taken usually is. There could be dead ends as we fine-tune with the whisperings of our own spirit, as we plunge back into ego-mind or thinking mode only to get reminded that meaning cannot be formulated. It is experienced in the most unexpected of moments, almost magic-like.

Future-Proofing Businesses

Seeds of progressive change have been planted generations before. For the scope of this book, we shall begin with Donella Meadows discussing systems thinking in 1972 and Karl Weick discussing sense making in 1995 and design thinking labs sprouting all over the globe in the early 2000s. The steps towards a more collaborative, meaning-making, and human-centred design focused world has been charted. Ownership of our planet, communities, and lives no longer remains separate. We are interconnected, and together we may reach our goals faster than if we went at it alone, as the African proverb goes.

The density of centuries past is purging even from our internal human systems, and it is time we let go of what no longer serves us and open to new knowledge, ideas, and values that can bring a sense of fulfilment like no other.

The confounded fears of system and even individual security systems collapsing are real and continue to reverberate until the change is made. This can excite us as a new chapter opens new pathways of being, interacting, and having a meaningful life. It will be jarring if we remain too quick to numb ourselves or distract ourselves until the issue hits home, affecting our mobility, livelihoods, and even community spaces: 'The blind spot would be to not see, not feel and not act'.[108] And each one of us has a role to play, going forward.

The collapses of our outer world may often be required to trigger an inner world self-destruct button so that we can embrace every single aspect of being a human again like when we were babies—all our fears, insecurities, vulnerabilities without judgement—and know that they do not define us. At the end of the day, we can overcome, we can keep rebuilding ourselves. And we must start this inner journey into ourselves to escape the duality we have grown to believe is our reality and truth.

As a collective, we are transitioning to a search for common ground now. To reconcile history's mistakes, make peace in the present, and dream of a harmonious future. Harmonising extremes will take time, and we will have to adopt *spectrum thinking*. This is a spiritually grounded practice for us to question with the intent to know but with four steps towards compassionate sharing at the same time. Information is not owed to us; neither do we have to beg or bribe for it. We may instead seek to understand what we can know by meeting the other halfway with our own vested interests. Aim here is to get to a state of heightened awareness of noticing both the said and unsaid in a room and to navigate cleverly to avoid stepping on any landmines and instead get closer to one's goal that meets the other person where they are at as well.

108 O. Scharmer, 'Turning Toward Our Blind Spot: Seeing the Shadow as a Source for Transformation', *Field of the Future Blog*, Medium, https://medium.com/presencing-institute-blog/turning-toward-our-blind-spot-seeing-the-shadow-as-a-source-for-transformation-aff23d480a55 (accessed 26 January 2024).

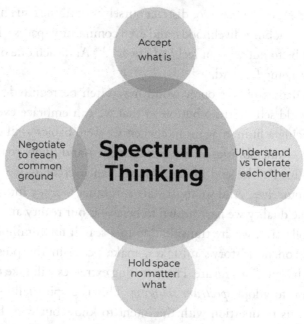

Figure 25: Four steps to spectrum thinking

This will not be achieved immediately. It will require personal willpower and mindset shifts on our end about how people are and why organisations are sometimes run 'badly'. Suspending judgement will be the first step and most difficult. Once surpassed, it gets easier. Once we individually start to claim back our own powers, we can reach this place of compassion for another, no matter how different they may seem in world view from us or how they may irritate us. It is best we lean into the growing diversity that makes up our world so that we can benefit from the richness of cross-pollination, interdisciplinary and intercultural ideation, informed from experience and real-world thinking.

The development of the Taskforce on Nature-Related Financial Disclosures (TNFD) is one such effort led by financial actors to address nature and biodiversity loss and hopefully reverse the financial exposure of companies from potential threats to related ecosystem-regulating services. For most of the century, we have operated in a linear take-waste-make manner; to expect nature's resources to be regenerative would be both unrealistic and unfair. This is especially so if we are not reversing the rate at which we are extracting or ensuring proper end-of-life treatment of waste, and depending on governments or industry associations to provide the infrastructure and regulation is too slow as well. Each actor is grappling with competing priorities as it is.

If we were to look at our business models and truly map out the resource, production, and waste streams of our products and services and subsequently map their cradle-to-grave journey, we can find circular economy solutions as shared in previous chapters. This could include reducing virgin-material sourcing or extraction, albeit it might come at a cost to retrieve used packaging from end users in the least-contaminated and timely manner to avoid production delays for future products. Further, capitalising on various green/sustainable financing loans to earn discounted interest rates and reporting progress on key sustainability performing indicators would be a win-win for financiers, shareholders, and employees alike.

Sustainable leadership here would mean leaders who understand we cannot know everything at once but need to know as much as we can, at least. They apply themselves to understanding challenges from an outside-in as much as an inside-in manner and help facilitate shifts towards possible common ground between conflicted parties or individuals/groups who just need a bit more information. Here, the impetus of a sustainable leader is to always stay neutral, provide a safe space for ideation and progressive thinking to bring people further along. A sustainable leader is therefore a knowledgeable individual working on honing their wisdom. This is the leadership required for a just transition.

Reflection Pointers:

- How are we storing our information and who knows most?
- Where are we in our own way when it comes to building our knowledge capabilities?
- Why are we losing crucial information we are unaware of?
- When are our people their best when it comes to information-sharing and how may we emulate and scale up these experiences?
- What are our norms of information sharing—do we encourage inter-business-unit collaborations or silo thinking?

- Who may we engage within our teams to steward cultural shifts required towards solving our sustainability challenges?
- How accurate are our sustainability data points and are they reported in real life by direct managers?
- Are our knowledge management systems well equipped to include learning and insights for new and senior employees?

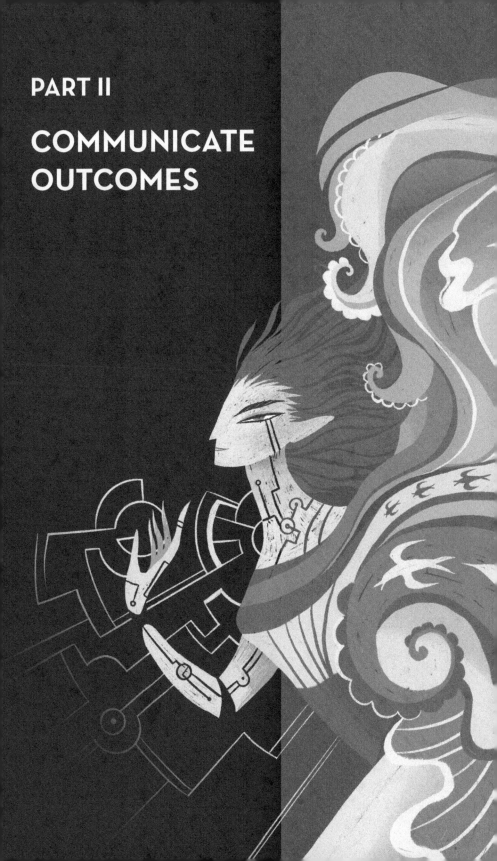

PART II

COMMUNICATE
OUTCOMES

IV

PRIORITISE PEOPLE

Shifting Our Focus To 'How' From 'Why'

In communicating action required, we need to look at the entire process of how we communicate. Most times, we do it piecemeal or as and when it is required. This is insufficient in building trust and our own awareness of how our organisations and families alike can achieve sustainable living and harmony.

Consistency and how we communicate matter most. Are we distracted, multitasking, half-present when making an ask? Or are we simply relaying an instruction we half-believe in and do not quite care if the other person understands or not? These are examples of unsuccessful communications that cause irritation, annoyance, and most importantly, dysfunction in our lives. The sooner we realise this, the quicker we can pivot to conscious communications that often come from an ironic state of being still and silent.

In *The Fifth Discipline*, Peter Senge elaborates on how 'new practices conflict with deeply held internal images of how the world works; images that limit us to familiar ways of thinking and acting. This is why we need to surface, test, and improve our internal pictures, assumptions and stories of how the world works'.[109] Often this is the roadblock to any change-management initiative. By uncovering the way critical decision-makers or stakeholders think and making them realise their own assumptions through an appropriate line of questioning, change can happen.[110] Another approach is to encourage 'bottom-line business accountability and think issues through for themselves through a variety of networks to keep connecting people to openly talk about problems and challenge each other's thinking'.[111]

Senge also points out the precise pain points when it comes to communication action needed—most people are motivated to preserve themselves from pain and threat that might emerge from having to learn and relearn, which he calls a skill incompetence.[112] There is however a myriad of ways to look at complex issues, and developing inquiry skills with face-to-face interactions to distinguish what is said from what is not is necessary in aligning intention and desired outcomes.[113] To avoid giving up, Senge recommends we start with revealing our own assumptions and reasoning to invite others to reciprocate so that we can identify what generalisations are in play and how we may move forward to learn together.[114]

Therefore, the intent is no longer 'I need to communicate my message' but rather 'How does the other person think so that I may get them to understand what I am trying to say?' in the hope that we can come to some common ground about the issue at hand. Now this shifts our approach from simply speaking to understanding, to working together for a desirable outcome, which may change if we realise better ways through discussion. Senge envisions that 'learning organisations of the future will make key decisions based on shared understandings of interrelationships and patterns of change', which makes sense.[115] If we are all looking at an elephant from different angles, we are for the better if we can all come together with the different pieces of information to build a more complete view.

---

[109]   P. Senge, *The Fifth Discipline: The Art and Practice of the Learning Organization* (revised and updated version), New York, Doubleday, 2006, p. 402, [**e-book**].

[110]   Senge, *The Fifth Discipline*, p.42-4.

[111]   Senge, *The Fifth Discipline*, p. 420.

[112]   Senge, *The Fifth Discipline*, p. 424.

[113]   Senge, *The Fifth Discipline*, p.402.

[114]   Senge, *The Fifth Discipline*, pp. 438-9.

[115]   Senge, *The Fifth Discipline*, p. 469.

When we communicate:	If the other party is hesitant or not interested:
Explain how we came to our view and the evidence for it	Ask them what is it about this conversation that makes it difficult to share openly
Ask if there is missing information that you should know	Discuss what can be done to overcome this barrier together
Listen if others have different views	Ask them what might change their view
Ask them to substantiate their view	Discuss if they could work together on a possible new direction

Table 2: Senge's advice to effective communications
and breaking deadlock

It is important to note the underlying expectations when it comes to empowering system actors to respect, honour, and uncover their vulnerabilities when it comes to partnering on change management required for collaboration in sustainability. Seeking and securing assurances in systems change therefore needs alignment and follow-through from the individual to organisational and systems change outcome intended. It is a two-way communication based on consistent feedback and trust building based on a suitable language between different entities. Investing in this process will ensure we are continuously moving and not taking two steps to take five back.

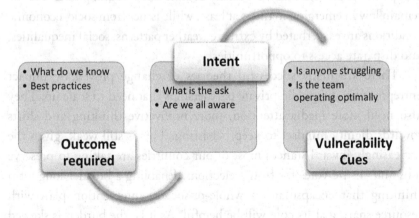

Figure 26: Working backwards from vision to drive mission

We are moving into a world with increased awareness of interconnections and tapping these intersectionalities to bolster cooperation and prosperity on a whole new level.

The Bigger Picture

Every organisation has its key stakeholders, individuals we are responsible to stay accountable to and who in turn contribute to the success and running of companies, governments, nonprofits. When we are focused on these stakeholders, it is easy to overlook the rest. This chapter is about noticing people are important. Some stakeholders have more power than others, but all are equally valid and important in value-chain engagements when it comes to sustainability. Constantly updating our own stakeholder lists and priority engagements will be crucial in building long-standing trust. Moreover, as disruptions and change remain, interdependencies between us and our stakeholders will also grow. There are adjacent possibilities to collaborating and partnering with the very entities that want us to succeed as well. With deliberation and action, the pathways can be paved for sustainable performance as a whole.

For societies, a just transition is a complex social phenomenon with many groups either falling through safety nets or needing more social protection to be included in the transitions towards the low-carbon and more digitised society we are in. Here, complementary partnerships and resource support schemes to provide basic services to uplift these marginal groups can prove necessary, especially as state budgets and public revenue remain low in emerging markets at least, while issues from socio-economic conditions are exacerbated by extreme weather patterns, social inequalities, and disparate access to opportunities.

There are many successful theories of change proven by impact entrepreneurs and public-private partnerships that need to scale up. They also need more media attention, more innovative thinking and shifts towards dignity mindset to keep persisting. This is still weak, given the increasingly inward stances most of our countries are taking to preserve jobs and ensure votes for future elections. Enabling a broader long-term thinking that encapsulates a whole-of-society intervention plan with resource sharing at its core will be helpful. As it is, the burden is skewed towards the public sector, with recent calls for private equity, developmental banks, sovereign wealth funds, pension funds, impact investors, venture capitalists to provide blended finance, especially where risk guarantees are assured for capital to flow to more risk-prone, unsustainable markets that need the urgent interventions towards sustainable development.

Just Transition For	Positive Societal Outcomes	Work With	Results
Low-income, rural communities	Patents for inventions that would otherwise go unnoticed	Industry R&D labs Institutions of higher learning	Access to protect one's intellectual property Continuous innovation and progressive growth for companies who partner Self-empowerment for the inventors
Academically inclined students from impoverished backgrounds	Access to fair and equitable education	Local schools Educators Digital learning solutions	Breaking out of poverty cycle Cultivating more talent to counter brain drain
Rural communities with limited access to skills development and jobs	Job creation and preservation of cultural heritage	Investors Local governments	Less push-pull factors for urbanisation Continuous development in rural areas
Rural communities with limited road/ mobile accessibility	Last-mile connectivity	Telecom munications providers Logistics companies Local entrepreneurs	Greater connectivity Disaster relief, market access especially via e-commerce
The unbanked	Microloans and debt financing for those with limited to no collateral	Platform providers National identification system Local banks Retail investors Aid agencies	Risk assurance (i.e. forex etc.) from local/ international funders End users can start their own ventures, achieve basic necessities, etc.

Table 3: Complementary partnerships that break vicious cycles

We need to share power with each other more than have power over one another, and reciprocal relationships are the bedrock since how we heal is fundamentally relational.[116] In *The Power of Collective Wisdom*, Alan

116 A. Briskin, S. Erickson and T. Callanan; J. Ott, *The Power of Collective Wisdom: And the Trap of Collective Folly*, San Francisco, Berrett-Koehler Publishers, 2009, p. 183 [e-book].

Briskin shares, 'We have the power with to harness our human imagination in the service of healthier institutions, new forms of cooperation, and more sophisticated ways of handling conflict. We have the power to heal the social chaos around us by creating fields of belonging'.[117]

Collective wisdom can emerge when we feel safe and challenged to find what is best in ourselves and the group in order to create our own community. This provides us with realisation that collaboration promotes learning, responsibility, and reward especially when we discover something larger than ourselves.[118] This mindset is growing prevalent, and the quicker we accept its beneficial prowess, the closer we can get to sharing responsibility and ownership over complex issues that need collective wisdom.

According to Donna Hicks, 'even when we are not speaking, we are communicating if someone is important or not . . . we need to pay more attention to the effect we have on others and dignity consciousness can help'.[119] She cites Harvard Business School research by Professor Amy Edmundson, who uncovered that a 'psychologically safe' environment in the workplace can increase learning and performance significantly as it predicts employees' engagement and quality of work produced.

But most leaders struggle with making it safe to be vulnerable in organisations.[120] In order to be vulnerable, trust needs to be present, and building transparency will be key. There will be a need to not just reveal problems but also solve them by tapping crowdsourced solutions as well as critiques. Accepting the challenges of operating in a reputation economy and pursuing sustainability in today's social media era where information gets viral, we will need to balance transparency, where some secrets will remain closeted.[121]

---

[117]   Briskin, Erickson and Callanan, *The Power of Collective Wisdom*, p. 181 [e-book].

[118]   Briskin, Erickson and Callanan, *The Power of Collective Wisdom*, p. 49.

[119]   D. Hicks, *Leading with Dignity: How to Create a Culture That Brings Out the Best in People*, New Haven, Yale University Press, 2018, p. 110 [e-book].

[120]   Hicks, *Leading with Dignity*, p. 111.

[121]   J. Hollender and B. Breen, *The Responsibility Revolution: How the Next Generation of Businesses Will Win*, San Francisco, Jossey-Bass, 2010, pp. 229-30 [e-book].

Stakeholder Capitalism

Sustainability as a concept is not new, although it seems new because of its accelerated interest and promotion spurred by the recent uptick in extreme weather patterns reporting drastic loss of lives and infrastructure damage. In fact, this is why developing nations are pushing for a loss-and-damages fund as they will be most impacted by the actions of developed countries from their historical emissions and fast-growing economies like China, India, and the US. The forecasted financial impact from stranding asset risks is in the hundred millions, causing insurers and reinsurers to review terms and raise premiums.

Even so, who is important is left to companies to decide.

The Global Reporting Initiative (GRI) is a disclosure standard that can help identify and responsibly account for different stakeholder types, including contracted workers, supply chain, and outdoor workers (if any). It is a valuable framework for mapping the important contributors to an organisation's functioning. However, no one is validating the claims unless independent assurers are hired, which comes at a cost, and they only verify information provided to them, try as they might to procure more information.

For the frontline managers, their important 'who' are the customers and vendors to keep business operating. For management, their important 'who' are their bosses, teams, and suppliers. For board members, their important 'who' are regulators, investors, and shareholders. For top management, their important 'who' would be financial analysts, media, shareholders, and investors. Keeping everyone informed, happy, and content is the real elephant in the room. And often, local communities are last in priority unless there is a compliance requirement.

There is an intricate balance between economy, governance, and fuelling business growth. Often, it comes at the expense of authenticity. Projection of power and keeping up appearances with strong marketing and advertising enables this facade to play out. Use the words *green*, *sustainable, engagement*—who is regulating?

The same in the philanthropy space—so much funds and donations are collected annually to fund various initiatives, and why are the inequality gaps not closing or not closing sooner?

Who is truly important is amiss again. We do not seem to really care unless it hurts our bottom line, but when will that be? When more lives are lost, communities facing dire repercussions from our contribution to biodiversity loss, environmental pollution, and/or ecosystem services disruptions? How effective are our mitigation and adaptation measures besides what the government is planning? How many of us are truly taking this seriously from a human-centred approach rather than an organisational survival perspective?

And for those of us who have read *Homo Sapiens*, corporations are just registered entities and not the people running it. If liabilities occur, it only impacts the entity, not the people. And this is something we have seen played out in lawsuits against corporations for causing grievous harm to communities, like the opioid addiction crisis in the US initiated by a pharmaceutical company.

The 1984 Bhopal gas leak is another similar incident, where legal loopholes and international jurisdictions deflected accountability from corporate headquarters to their local operations. Much the same as developers with outsourcing scope of responsibility to their main contractors and their subcontractors. Who is really responsible for the worker is hard to say. And such power dynamics in a highly unregulated space call for ethical reflections on our end.

In *Demanding Sustainability*, John Morrissey and Patrick Heidkamp share a five-pillar framework to consider, map out, and plan for just transitions in policymaking, community organising, and corporate social responsibility: an ecological prosperity, decarbonised economy, shared burden (costs), transformative social sustainability, and just resilience. But how willing are we to go to such lengths?

Identity politics has also been front and centre of many conflicts and progressive measures at the same time. Looking at affirmative action in post-apartheid South Africa, I could see how there was a need to bridge the education gap, for instance. Yet as an exchange student there, I could also see the failings of such a systemic approach as there was a lack of jobs waiting for campus-filled black South Africans who matriculated thanks to this system. The class divide was also apparent in my classes as I hardly interacted with South African blacks in my theatre, politics, and visual studies courses. Living in Pretoria, I also witnessed this on my weekly commute to the township of Mamelodi, where I was greeted by primary school children from the neighbouring slum area with little access to resources due to poverty and violence in their communities.

I still recall my first day of orientation, when the school principal received news that a student's father had passed away the night before because of a fire caused by his neglect after having one too many drinks. The student lost not only their father but also their home. And the principal responded with a detachment that still haunts me today, almost as if this was expected and part of a regular day.

Nelson Mandela's prison cell at Robben Island was another eye-opening experience. The prejudices of discrimination can either break us or build us up stronger, and it is here where I saw the small cell he lived in for eighteen years and the impact he went on to make after. To me, 2009 South Africa still looked divided, and Shakira was rallying the troops that World Cup: 'Waka waka, this time for Africa'.

All of us represent a certain cultural identity or background. While two people from the same ethnic background could not be more different in personality, preferences, and lifestyle, the truth is, there is still a common thread that binds them. This is not the same as someone completely from a different cultural background trying to assimilate.

Yet it is not difficult to shift this expectation to realise there is more richness to be had when we are open to what another has to offer. It is often fear that is stopping us or some limiting belief that only our way could be possibly right—what does the other know? And this we have to transcend if we are to solve more complex issues that will come as we advance in technology and its related risks and considerations. Trust is not inherently there for most people. This comes with world views and life experiences as well as beliefs passed onto us from our environments and the company we keep. This is where I find left-right politics a little disconcerting as it can verge on extremism if taken too far, on either end.

How Do We Reassure
The Poor, Vulnerable, And Marginalised?

We are at Ani Choying's concert at the Sydney Opera House. She is ethereal: the singing nun from Nepal. Fast-forward a few months, I am spinning prayer wheels at the Boudhanath Stupa in Kathmandu. My sister snaps a picture of me from the back. Fast-forward, now my course mates and I are at the immigration office to extend our Nepalese student visas. There is a Canadian nun in maroon robes, looking visibly distressed. Noticing we were the only other foreigners, we connect. She is high-strung; it has been a long and unexplainable wait for her. Former military, she found a home in Kathmandu Valley, yet has to make the dreaded yearly visit into the city to extend her right to stay. We part ways as my professor exits. It is unclear what was said in that room, but we got our student visa, it seems. We leave relieved.

Similarly, I am at the Zimbabwean customs. The officer very seriously looked up and asked in a deep-throated voice whose passport this is. I literally gulped as my red passport appeared, and meekly raised my hand. I did not know anyone in Zimbabwe except that Mugabe was a frequent flyer to Singapore for his medical treatments and had a strong friendship with Lee Kuan Yew. The officer looked at me again after checking the photo and then broke into a wide white grin. 'You go for free', and he returned my USD20. I could not have been more relieved. Going through customs anywhere is always intimidating.

As such, access to services is key, with proper determinant factors that one is not being exploited, cheated, or compromised with the choices they make. That is primarily the number one fear that needs to be countered when offering social protection. Social protection is not charity or ensuring good corporate social responsibility. These efforts, while commendable, do not lend dignity to the stakeholders involved. In fact, it either fuels a dependency complex or an inferiority complex that breeds resentment especially for oneself being in a state of relying instead of being self-reliant.

In this section, we want to discuss how we can make systems more self-reliant and, in doing so, the individuals that make them. The truth is that there is a discrepancy with the way we function in society. Charity, benevolence, and corporative giving are part of a culture where the giving comes from a place of privilege. In recognising this privilege, we fail to understand how this privilege came to be and how instead we can make contexts around us more equitable to begin with, because we can.

This will require a disruption in the charity, giving space but only in terms of upgrading the way we think and function as a whole so that we empower the other instead of breed codependency.

Here the giver is also codependent on this dynamic because it is always a two-way process. Giving requires a receiver, and the receiver validates the role of the giver. It is an endless cycle. And what happens when the theory of change is incomplete or not sustained? Then the target group are left to their own devices, this time worse off than before because the safety nets that were extended to them are no longer there or they never learnt how to be independent.

We are not advocating for a complete 'pull the rug from under the feet of the individual' solution. That would be cruel but instead a gradual upliftment by incremental support mechanisms that ensure the individual and therefore family unit, community is well supported to function towards achieving outcomes for themselves.

This is observable in developing economies dependent on foreign aid too. Once the aid runs out or a crisis like the pandemic occurs, local communities are left to fend for themselves, and the worrisome thing is the aid only helps equip them to some extent—they have to relearn many old ways of being to adapt to new challenges.

The tendency to avoid being independent is also there. It is definitely easier to accept help, receive support, and go with prescribed intervention for our well-being. This means we do not have to think or can simply trust the other to guide us, as they have others, towards a better well-being index. However, this is not self-reliance, and it puts us in a coop, along with many others. We are each unique beings with unlimited potential. What interventions should aim to do is offer an enabling environment to support the growth of this potential regardless of demographic group or geographical location.

For example, youth from low-income single-household families in urban Mumbai may have varied dreams and aspirations, but all that is dashed when there is limited access or ability to attain education, much less to dream. This is clearly shown in the Netflix documentary by the

Shanti Bhavan organisation in South India. This is an initiative that has approached the issue of lack of access with an intervention method: talent scout and support each family with onboarding one child into the sponsored education system so that they may complete schooling and pursue higher education, to attain better paid jobs and support their families in turn.

While this is a commendable theory of change for an education intervention programme, it however also shows limitations in achieving a full set of outcomes that are desirable by the organisation because the individual is unique. Answerable to donors and its own outcome metrics, the programme tries its best to mentor the graduates into making smart decisions, and realise how much more of a challenge this is when the support structures of home in regards to familial expectations for the graduate to succeed are low/unhelpful/dependent on survival. The theory of change may need more partners, more attention to details that creep up unexpectedly. These are insights we only get when we make a start, and that is the most crucial step of it all. We all need to start, no matter how small, and build from there.

Target Groups	Key Objectives	Results	Requirements	Stakeholders Involved
Homeless	Housing Food Jobs Schools (if there are kids) Overcoming addictions, mental health, debts, etc.	Sustained employment	Trusted accountability partners

Suitable job placements with transparent disclosure

Holistic support with caregiving | NGOs to develop 'theory of change' road map for clients

Work with local employers and government agencies to fund job placements while providing holistic intervention on a mid-/long-term basis |

Marginalised groups (i.e. outcaste, informal workers, caregivers, etc.)	Breaking out of poverty cycle Eradicating social discrimi nation Regulated informal-sector wages	Able to contribute back to the economy, advance socially and progress	Boarding with meals and focused academic attention coupled with safe transitions back home	Institutes of learning, nonprofits dedicated to education, ministry of education, foreign donors
Youth who lack skills, knowledge and access	Lower unemploy ment rate Increase employa bility rate	Youth are suitably employed and contri buting to society	Job redesign and culture discussions especially for existing firms	Institutions of higher learning (IHLs) and businesses to work together to understand and redesign jobs in emerging sectors (i.e. sustainability, gig economy, etc.)
Local communities	Regene ration of resources otherwise misma naged or depleted; new economic opportu nities, societal upliftment	Reduced exodus, more development and resilient communities	Policy shifts, resource provision, consultation and bottom-up engagement by local community (i.e. town-hall meetings, etc.)	Political parties, grassroots committees, local governments

Table 4: Thematic Social Protection Floors Required

Now, how can impact investing/corporate giving and sustainability reporting converge to such a point that they enable communities to become self-reliant without compromising business goals but bolstering them instead?

Create a theory of change that is forward-looking with real-time data inputs to chart plausible futures and help steer investment towards meaningful outcomes that offer risk guarantees especially to the most vulnerable populations so that they may thrive and, as a consequence, offer exponential returns on investment (ROI).

The science behind this is not difficult. How can we all become truly self-reliant is something most of us in the developed world are achieving with the help of mindfulness, self-help, and life coaching. We know this ensures optimal performance and well-being beyond hustling, striving, and managing lives' daily tasks. How then can we ensure others can also get on this track? And why, you may ask, should this be our individual concern in the first place—which is fair. The truth is we do not exist alone. We often have to get going in life with the existence or help of others. What we all experienced during the pandemic is testimony to the fact that when one country goes into lockdown, we are inevitably affected either directly or indirectly.

Perhaps our food-supply chains were restricted, or we no longer could meet business partners, friends, or family. Losing our freedom to travel, transact, and predict is a vulnerable place to be. We enforce this vulnerability by assuming we remain separate as we transit out of the global crisis of 2020. This is not the end though because climate risks are affecting infrastructure, assets, and public health. Going forward, we need to remember we coexist with others. Adopting flexible mindsets to encourage others besides ourselves to anchor down important values for harmony, collaboration, and future resilience-building is all the more crucial now.

Offering reciprocal and dignified exchange of knowledge from and between communities and business interests is a strong precondition for sustainability. Hyperlocalised understanding of community needs is often a good-to-have and not so much a must-have due to business priorities and limited bandwidth. Ensuring required data is collected and mapped systematically and integrated into workflow charts or reports seamlessly in line with international reporting standards makes a strong case for businesses to consider this investment.

Hyperlocalised apps customised for low bandwidth and language-challenged markets can help collect data through local stakeholder partnerships and flow directly to a subscribed client's workflow integration plug-in with self-managed notifications on capital market, risk factor, governance, social unrest, and environmental updates. This allows frontline risk managers and business operations teams to work on cross-functional partnerships to advance resilience goals for their company, further ensuring buy-in from board and executive management on service delivery enhancements are in alignment with sustainability reporting mechanisms and business profit margins.

Quantifying qualitative data to business dollar value is not too far from becoming mainstream as the focus shifts towards reporting and aligning corporate initiatives with social responsibility, and country regulations like the Modern Slavery Act, regional/international law as well as standards bodies like the Global Reporting Initiative (GRI) and International Integrated Reporting Council (IIRC). More and more regulators are asking for mandatory reporting.

How to transcend the conundrum of underreporting or mandatory tokenism (greenwashing, for instance) reporting requires a dedicated effort in understanding the purposes behind these different reporting requirements, followed by the business value it brings to your enterprise and what it means for the mid- to long-term viability of customer engagement, ceteris paribus. This is a cross-functional effort and one that requires leadership from senior management to guide and build clarity together. The different requirements do not have to confound us into anxiety or freeze mode. If we all take some time to understand what each model looks at and the value creation for your business model, the benefit can surpass consistent striving mode.

Gaining an overview and where a business stands on reporting measures can help understand its impact on communities/markets. There could be an instance where current business value proposition lacks any alignment with the 2030 Sustainable Development Goals (SDGs). Instead of status quo, local partnerships can be easily sourced to kick-start your SDG or ESG (economic, social, and governance) footprint mapping journey for the business. Furthermore, with many established database solutions available, businesses can start building their stakeholder community from the platform, identifying customer needs and engagement gaps and opportunities to pivot and strengthen their business market position. Last-mile traceability is also made easier with blockchain.

The parallel reality is that reporting alone is insufficient if it does not meaningfully engage local stakeholders on the ground. This takes time; it requires a concerted effort to track and monitor data coming in and ensure engagement campaigns with customers are meaningful and not annoying. Most times, enterprise teams have limited manpower, and this gets overlooked. Community data also needs to be collected consistently over time, and honest evaluation of what works and what does not requires adequate internal feedback loops set up within organisations as well as a culture that looks at such feedback constructively and not personally.

Culture therefore becomes an important topic to address, and if not aligned, it can lead to deadlocks internally despite board decisions or senior management decisions to align with sustainability reporting. Managing the shift from pure financial metrics of profit-making to incorporating business impact on non-financial metrics requires education, realignment and adopting mechanisms that support this transition. Sustainability reporting teams or reporters alone or the CEO will not suffice.

Reflection Pointers:

- Do you agree that new ways of helping each other out of our socio-economic dilemmas are required?
- How aware are organisations about their contributions to society that generate the returns on social values, branding, and most importantly, impact?
- Who could be important that we are not including at the moment?
- How robust is my materiality assessment and does it provide me with sufficient information on value-adding my sustainability performance and priorities?
- Where are the opportunities to partner and broaden impact when it comes to community upliftment projects?
- What theory of change does my organisation want to support?
- When should we expect the outcomes of our impact investment to percolate and in what forms?
- How are we reporting stakeholder engagements, findings, and contributions in our communications? Is this important?

V

LEADERS WHO SUCCEED

Talented people, in the right kind of culture, have better ideas,
execute those ideas better, and even develop other people better.[122]
- *The Responsibility Revolution: How the Next
Generation of Businesses Will Win*

Creativity ↑

| Be **present** to witness the *opportunities* that arise from potential risks to **mobilise** people effectively and *progress* | **Provide** time and safe spaces for *different* ideas and *perspectives* to be **shared** to increase *value creation* from stakeholders |

Stagnation ↓

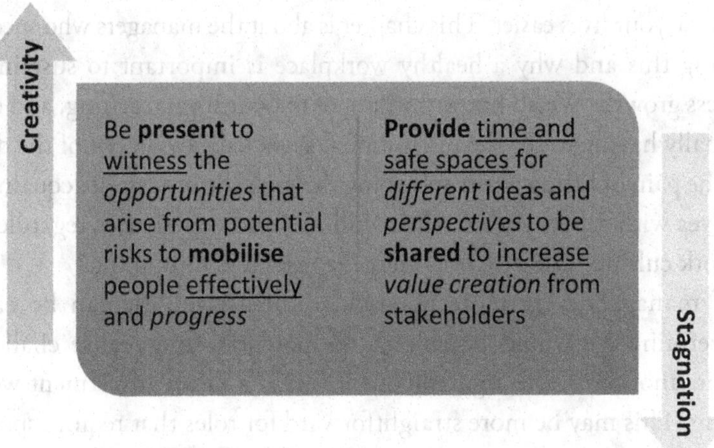

Figure 27: Overview of this chapter's objectives

---

[122] J. Hollender and B. Breen, *The Responsibility Revolution: How the Next Generation of Businesses Will Win,* San Francisco, Jossey-Bass, 2010, p. 163 **[e-book]**.

F irst, I would say because you are reading this, you are successful because you chose yourself and chose to learn. These two qualities are what helps leaders be a good leader. Here, *good* refers to what subordinates like myself would want in a leader: kindness, fairness, and receptivity. Kindness to know when others are struggling and when it is OK to keep pushing deliverables. Fairness in how we treat all because it makes a difference to morale and everything always comes full circle. If your turnover is high, this could be one of the reasons. Lastly, receptivity to understand and accept that none of us know everything and we hire to get ourselves out of that rut, so trust in the talent's abilities and facilitate the growth and learning journeys of everyone instead of worrying if you come across like you know everything or not.

Having said this though, there are many other factors why firms are affected by high turnover, and this will not be covered here. Some examples include job-expectation mismatch, cultural challenges, change of career focus, and more. These aspects are hard to govern as it is subjective and dependent on the needs and preferences of both employers and employees that may not get adequately covered in rounds of interviews and probationary assessment. Often this comes with time, exposure, and individual timeline plans.

Nevertheless, for leaders, there is scope to work with those who stay and make your lives easier. This chapter is about the managers who succeed in doing this and why a healthy workplace is important to sustainable business growth. We all know the pain of onboarding, teaching, and then eventually having to see the institutional knowledge walk out of the door, with the pain of hiring again and going through the process of acquainting ourselves with a new person, their skill sets and experiences regardless if the work culture is diverse or homogeneous. Fit is important.

If managers were more assured of themselves, fit can be easier to ascertain. We would be able to see potential and realise challenge areas in another before figuring out if this is a talent investment worth making. This may be more straightforward for roles that require specific qualifications and experiences, and it's just a matter of finding the most suitable graduate or credentials. As we undergo the low-carbon transition and push towards more green skills in all job functions, some nuances need to be thought over.

Grounding Priorities In Sustainability

As managers and leaders, our first priority is to ensure work gets done and done by relevantly skilled people (ideally). Sometimes this is not the case and leads to much frustration at the working level. It is here that the leader needs to be able to read talent accurately based on how they perform and not what they say they can do. There is a difference, and it will save leaders time to evaluate this carefully:

a) Are we meeting our deliverables on time?
b) What is the roadblock or hurdle that is disrupting our progress?
c) How may we mitigate or work around it?

Once we figure out the cause, and if it is personnel related, it is best to exercise kindness to find out their challenge. With so much information coming at us sometimes with emails and interpersonal challenges, not all workers are adept at managing it all even if they look like they are. If there is a delay, observe further even if they reply with 'everything is OK'. How do they look, what is the state of affairs with their other correspondences, and how are fellow team members responding? These subtle cues can unearth more information. Keep checking in on the issue at hand and take note of the frequency of occurrences. More than once is a red flag that personnel are struggling and other forms of intervention may need to be considered.

Perhaps your schedule does not allow such luxuries as following up on team members to this extent. Then the next question is, what are we busy with and what is the return of investment from the various tasks and activities we are engaged in? If we sit and evaluate our schedules filled with meetings with limited to no outcomes or with further follow-ups, we are not using our finite time well and at the expense of building a healthy workplace.

What is a healthy workplace? Yes, eating well and being able to move, stand, exercise together are as important as a psychologically safe workplace. Here the topic might get a little sensitive and rightly so because most of us are not even aware of our own mental health. We neglect it to help others or dismiss it to pursue more urgent tasks or distractions.

Managers who succeed have a stronghold on their own mental health. They know at any given time what stress they are facing, why, and how to manage it. They know very well not to displace it on others and to ask for space when needed. They schedule sufficient time for self-care daily and ensure team members can do the same by optimising productivity during the workday so that time avails before or after work to pursue sports and other hobbies.

The best workplaces are ones that offer reminders to take time off for family and provide sufficient activities to move, network, and build social connections. Just planning an event is insufficient though. Following through with the intent for employees to break the ice and feel belonging in the workplace takes organic magic. It is best established bottom-up, and as such, firms may offer budgets for groups of employees to apply for, in order to pursue healthy workplace-related activities—like a sunset jog or walk around the central business district, volunteering to teach other colleagues gardening, or cooking leftover food. These are ideas sustainable companies are implementing and doing well in. Ensuring healthy workplaces has never been more than a priority now since the global pandemic.

Successful managers understand and value the optimisation of productivity over clocking the hours and some overtime to appear hard-working and secure the next performance appraisal. This culture is discouraging to employees who need time and flexibility to be creative and contribute innovative ideas to the workplace. It also devalues the quality of work as individuals take longer to complete it rather than be productive about it. This does not mean that more work needs to be assigned if a team completes it faster now.

Vision and linking it to the overall business strategy and goals are crucial. Every function has a purpose and importance in an organisation, especially in the green transition. Resource optimisation will be necessary as most if not all of us race to net zero. Carbon emissions reduction and related energy, water, waste cost savings from procurement to operations, to waste management and scope 3 liabilities need to play a part. This requires the departmental vision to be clear, precise, and linked to the business's decarbonisation road map. Simply assigning a sustainability performance target to a frontline worker is inadequate. The team needs to understand why and how they can achieve it especially if reductions of any kind have been difficult to achieve prior.

Successful managers understand these complexities are often personality related. They inspire rather than provoke and ensure collective success is possible especially if the sustainability directive has been largely top-down driven. They come well prepared with assurances to guide the team towards a plausible direction. They request feedback as the team journeys together to meet their quarterly targets. Where the targets may be lagging, successful managers are proactive and address them head-on rather than avoid or skirt around the issue until management requests for specifics. They are honest about negative disclosures and do not make individual feel alone.

By role-modelling this attitude, leaders can strengthen the psychological safety of workplaces and grant dignity to themselves and individuals. Cultures where this is not possible need not stay stuck. Work structures can help with the change management, such as reporting lines can shift towards ESG committees instead of direct supervisor. In a broader inter-business unit, these challenges can be openly shared among peers who may undergo similar experiences, with problem-solving and clarity more attainable. This then builds confidence within teams to execute their work well and hit the next quarterly target.

Leaders appreciate robust monitoring and tracking dashboards to analyse the trends in their sustainability and decarbonisation plans. As this is a trust and brand-building exercise essentially, successful managers understand that progress is not linear all the time and make allowances for sudden changes or disappointing performance. They make resilience plans and leverage on alternative work streams or business functions to compensate. Most importantly, leaders know that because sustainability is intricately interwoven within the business, it will take a value-chain effort to decarbonise over time even if a portfolio approach is taken over an equity or operational approach. Creating more opportunities for overall carbon savings will benefit the business with future investments in carbon offsets or taxes, depending on which direction climate policies will take.

Regulation need not scare us, and the leader is aware that compliance, while important, is just one piece of the motivational puzzle. Successful managers transcend compliance and create meaning behind pursuing business goals for sustainability. The means to the end is evidence-based rather than emotional, grounded in business operational challenges over need to satisfy external-facing stakeholders, and coached in positive growth mindsets.

Sustainability, healthier workplaces, and business viability in the long haul with emerging financial risks from disruptions related to cyber, climate, regulation can be achieved with persistence. The successful manager knows that timelines may be beyond anyone's tenure and will require successors to follow through as well. Making targets as granular as possible and easy to implement and track will be necessary. Technology solutions that aid in providing business intelligence and asset-level detail will be handy. Leaders appreciate the multitude of options and leverage them cleverly to optimise their and their team's productivity goals.

Managers who succeed never stop learning. They grow their networks, understand the latest industry trends, and always hold space and compassion for where they are at and where they can be through realistic approaches. No one can decarbonise overnight or achieve an audacious dream, but it starts with clear intention and a vision that makes strategic sense. This is not easy. Sometimes, the best way may not be a linear reduction right away. It may be a business-as-usual until we aggregate enough funds to invest in the time-saving, business-useful technologies or wait for first movers to attempt, to leverage their best practice.

Co-creating sustainable business outcomes for immediate stakeholders and secondary value-chain partners also requires an integrated planning approach. This is where joint committees led by a C-suite member with board buy-in may help to crystallise and ensure all business units are able to work together towards common ground. Whilst our realities may be mired with more crucial business priorities such as meeting product delivery timelines and managing customers, the value in investment time to strategise with inputs from across the board is necessary. The inertia might be high, so take the time to keep lobbying for it.

There is a tangible benefit in an integrated approach. Successful managers know this well. They understand the intricacies of varying business demands. They are able to map out the priorities and chart the best plan forward in decarbonising. With good preparation and waiting to respond when all the chips fall in place, the successful manager keeps fine-tuning the pathways to sustainability with high-level plans for board and top management, and more granular charts and figures for working teams. Meanwhile, they openly communicate this to teams involved to keep morale up as patience is a virtue we all need, especially in the fast-paced and timeline-sensitive worlds we live in.

The vertical and horizontal understanding of business integration puts the successful manager in a formidable position to embed sustainability, healthy workplaces, and resilience across the board.

With all engines, emergency equipment, activity decks, aft, mid-ships. and more well engaged, cruise ships still sail with much caution to the prevailing circumstances and changing weather patterns. Nevertheless, if safeguards are in place and everyone plays their part on the ship, anomalies are rare and everyone has a relatively good time. There are no guarantees, and leaders know this. When possible, they aim for guarantees via the low-hanging fruit.

What are the low-hanging fruit when it comes to healthier workplaces, for instance? Staff satisfaction varies, with some requiring being heard, seen, and acknowledged and others needing perks or benefits to sustain their interest in staying. Most, if not all, appreciate autonomy and trust from their leaders that they are doing their job and that they can deliver in time. There are some recalcitrant who may misuse this trust and make appearances. The low-hanging fruit to ensure guarantee of commitment by workers lies in the leadership's accountability mechanisms.

How are we being accountable with one another? What is the level of transparency we share and how are we reporting progress, successes, mistakes with each other? In other words, how aware is the leader of what is happening and their ability to nip issues in the bud rather than letting them fester? Avoiding the making of a toxic environment is the first guarantee leaders can strive for to ensure healthier workplaces have a fighting chance to stay and enrich both the employees and company bottom line.

According to Jeffrey Hollender in *The Responsibility Revolution*, 'too many stellar corporate citizens fail to meet the minimum requirement that fully engage associates' hearts and minds'. In fact, there is a need to create a dynamic, inclusive environment that frees people to give their all. Workplaces may operate like communities where profits fuel the drive to fulfil a larger purpose. These places appreciate individual accomplishments by enabling visibility to work and outcomes that are often intangible to be seen by management through peer performance review. Feedback is available for top management, and staff can set their own strategic direction as an intrapreneur.

Consistent company growth is more important than short-term gains in market share or profits.[123] It helps when company's growth vision and values are internalised by employees. Innovation depends on people, which leads to 'enduring, superior performance' and 'innovative ideas can spring from any part of the organisation'.[124]

Additionally, successful managers understand the need for education or awareness—not detailed research or reports but simple marketable language for why their business is sustainable, planning to decarbonise, and how to socialise other teams to get on board, especially employees facing customers. This language may not come easily, but it can be co-created with other teams via the ESG committee for example, for everyone to own. The most important point is to stay aligned, even as market shifts occur.

The Threat Of The Triple Ds

Delays, delusions, and disclosures—they may not seem related; nevertheless, they can be in our way as successful managers. Let's discuss delays first. It is not in the human psyche to expect the unexpected, much less delays, when delays are actually more common than we like. It happens just because sometimes, or because of a fault in the system or a kink. It often triggers us to react instead of respond, and in the case of ensuring progress, we may take drastic action to upend as well, which could be detrimental to our mental health and that of others.

So let us take a step back. How are we planning our time and projects and plans with buffer set aside? What are our assumptions that something can be delivered in said amount of time? There might be historical data to

---

[123] J. Hollender and B. Breen, *The Responsibility Revolution: How the Next Generation of Businesses Will Win,* San Francisco, Jossey-Bass, 2010, pp. 162-3 [**e-book**].

[124] Hollender and Breen, *The Responsibility Revolution,* p.212.

show previous successes, but most times, we are going with hunches and depending on how well we really know our own capabilities and that of others; this can backfire if we overestimate or are assured a project can be delivered in said amount of time. This is where we need to harness our abilities to see things as they are, overcome any sense of powerlessness in questioning or requesting further information, and own our discernment in order to operate undisrupted.

As simple as this sounds though, most times we are clouded by delusions (not in a bad way). We all project our inner worlds to the real world we live in, whether we know it or not. Some of us may have better self-control than others and not show it as much, but over time, it does start to manifest despite the shells of being we hold on to in defence. This is human nature and to be expected. Successful managers understand this aspect of human defence where we each want to protect our own ego and identity constructs in order to exist in the world as successfully as we can.

The only issue is, when we project, we sometimes wish for an ideal situation or limit the potential in a situation based on our own individual world views and lenses of making sense of this world. This is conditioning and exposure from childhood and over life that cannot be changed overnight. It takes a certain personality dedicated to tremendous self-growth to recognise this tendency of the ego and to carefully mine the feedback we receive from others to tweak our projections on the world. The best would be to keep practising vipassana to see things as they are or any other mindfulness practice. The beauty of such a practice is that it reminds us to stay focused on one thing at a time, and by giving it our full attention and presence, we can take in all the tangible and subtle information otherwise missed when we are multitasking.

Often someone being deluded by projecting a limited impression or perspective of an issue is reliving an uncomfortable experience from the past where they were most likely told to internalise this for reasons unknown to us. This is why managers who succeed practise mindfulness and empathy, which may not be our cup of tea, and we keep at it to keep ourselves sane.

Truth is, a lot of management is managing people's inner worlds projected on situations that present unique challenges that can be easily handled with either a top-down directive or a clear objective. We miss hearing the inner turmoil or listen too much to it to make sense of whether we are making the best decision or not. An evidence-based approach is always the best, and this is where some objectivity can be derived. Successful managers are therefore careful with the approaches they use when sharing directives and help find the purpose behind the task for their team in order to deliver a desired outcome. This brings everyone along instead of isolating or creating confusion by allowing projections to linger and eventually fester when a project messes up.

Moving away from blame and shame is crucial these days as more of us grow in awareness of our own mental health. Like physical health, blame and shame has an impact on our self-esteem, psyche, and trust-building mechanisms with the world. When we feed more negative information readily available, especially if we have cognitive biases that approve this thinking, we risk devaluing ourselves eventually. Because the world is such and such, and therefore people behave such and such, this must be the outcome, which will never change and therefore we are stuck with this melancholy—no. This is a vicious cycle we can unplug from once successful managers notice and correct the impressions that lead team members to feel and respond this way. And it starts with moving away from blaming and shaming.

Yes, there are times when the culprit is clearly sabotaging the deliverable with unhealthy patterns such as procrastination and pleasing others by agreeing to take on more. This is often not in the control of others, to apprehend the culprit from avoiding such behaviour. It is where the successful manager can help create a culture of reasonableness and see things as they are instead of allow such delusions to occur. The culprit is unaware of his or her own abilities and having internalised that pleasing the boss is important in one's progression in life, they agree to more than they can chew in order to survive. Others see this as inauthentic, and it promotes gossip and unhealthy social behaviour, which can bring morale and others' expectations and self-esteem down if not caught early by the manager. In fact, in some situations it could have a multiplier effect where more start practising such behaviours with little work being done and more excuses for conflict resolutions instead.

Redefining *Busy*

The manager is busy but not with productive tasks. And in some worst-case scenarios, ignoring or avoiding resolving such conflicts is most detrimental to team harmony. Leaving the issue to resolve itself does not happen. Resentment and revenge mode kick in instead, and it is the manager who eventually suffers with poor deliverables or more backbiting, which they have to accept in the form of bullying, sarcasm, and humiliation through daily banter and discussions. These backhanded comments are usually ignored by managers who are unable to cope. Instead, they project a 'benefit of the doubt' version of themselves in order to resolve the situation, and this just encourages unhealthy attitudes and behaviour to grow while productive, creative, and proactive action takes the bench. The team culture has taken a turn for the worse, and we wonder what has happened.

Successful managers prioritise building trust and safety, always. This is not a one-off or ad-hoc exercise, it is a daily commitment towards building a healthy work culture where all can thrive and not just the usual people who shine. It requires a clear acknowledgement that we all have worth regardless of our job titles and fundamentally everyone ought to be treated with dignity. Respect is built as we acknowledge each other's dignity with appropriate actions—being professional in our speech, including others where conversations are work-related, and being aware that others' opinion can be helpful and we need not get on the defensive.

With so much of our inner worlds showing up to work, family gatherings, and social events, it is difficult to keep it hidden. In fact, the more accepting we become of this connection to our inner world, the better we will be. Why and how we respond is usually because of the state our inner world is in, which has been influenced by factors and time-space continuums before the present moment. This is not meant to confound us. With practising mindfulness and reflections through journaling or self-talk, we can start this journey into our inner worlds.

This is where the disclosures can get confusing, and the ethics behind it. What would be a good amount of information to disclose and what should we not disclose? How important is disclosure and is it possible not to disclose anything?

These are all thoughts that would have passed through our minds at some point or another—it is human nature. As successful managers, we are first aware of the business boundaries and requirements for strict compliance. Sustainability is an ever-growing space with even more disclosures to come as we start to understand its complexities and interconnectedness to upstream and downstream impacts on business operations. From the internal stakeholder to external, disclosure extent will vary, and how it is communicated also varies.

We often err on the 'safer' side with the most minimal or strategically worded information, often convoluted in how it is written because of legacy or strict adherence to communications protocol; we avoid what needs to be said in the clearest way possible to bring people along with us.

It is not disclosure that is important but rather, the value of transparency and exercising it with our stakeholders to build trust, which is important. When we know that we can safely ask questions and read about a company's sustainability practices, we feel assured that we are factored in the business and that the business values building trust with its value chain. These efforts are important as more and more feel the effects of a warming planet and extreme weather patterns. The tendency to want to put the blame for such occurrences on some entity is escalating, and in due course, businesses of all sizes will be affected if we miss out on building trust in the communities we operate in.

In *The Power of Framing* by Gail T. Fairhurst, she shares the work of ethicists James Anderson and Elaine Englehardt, who propose that how we make ethical choices begins with how we feel responsible towards each other. If there is a high sense of responsibility, then we will carefully evaluate how to act. This is why, when it comes to compliance, strict protocols and standard operating procedures need to be followed with suitable verification and validation standards to uphold accuracy of reporting.

By communicating ethically, Gail shares, we 'enhance human worth and dignity by fostering truthfulness, fairness, responsibility, personal integrity, and respect for self and others'.[125] As such, it is important for us to accept the consequences of our actions, including communications,

---

[125]   G. Fairhurst, *The Power of Framing: Creating the Language of Leadership*, 2nd edition, San Francisco, Jossey-Bass, 2010, p. 246, [e-book].

and expect the same for others. Such a code of conduct helps us manage confusion that often arises from vague instructions or information a manager tells one team member to relay to the rest, which may suffer misrepresentation when it finally gets relayed to the team, leading to more upsets and confusion and time wasted on the managers' end as they attempt to de-conflict or avoid the blame altogether.

Communicating responsibly shapes the identity of an organisation, not just the individual. Successful managers diligently promote what this means and act ethically to grow the team accordingly.[126] Once again, mindfulness is key here, as well as time and self-awareness. The successful manager observes, reflects, and ensures the organisation is progressive. This need not be based on a sense of morality, as it is subjective. Instead, framing from a responsibility perspective is more useful in showing how we could all act with each other. For this, we need to 'focus on the who, what, when, where and why details of the framing involved', and leaders need to understand what the design problem is.[127]

According to Peter Senge, systems thinking expert, organisations that are unable to see how they operate and how they are interconnected structurally may not be that free. Mental models might be contributing to silo thinking for those involved.[128] If we can understand the patterns, we are able to see the risk factors that lead to certain outcomes without assigning blame to anyone and, rather, identifying which situations might be contributing to unhealthy workplace culture, leadership, and more.[129]

In summary, how each of our organisations are governed and structured may differ. This has different avenues for successful management as well as its own set of challenges. A mindful leader is aware of the system, its complexities and possibilities to contribute to unhealthy work cultures. Attuned to the the dignity® approach, a successful manager ensures ethical communications and frameworks are in place for teams to practise and embody. There is no perfect situation or leadership, and we can get as close

126 Fairhurst, *The Power of Framing*, p. 250 [e-book].
127 Fairhurst, *The Power of Framing*, p. 279.
128 Fairhurst, *The Power of Framing*, p. 331.
129 JH. Lee, BA. Aubert, JR. Barker, Risk mapping in community pharmacies. *Journal of Patient Safety and Risk Management*. 2023; 28(2): 59–67. DOI: 10.1177/25160435231154167.

to it as possible by being mindful and building our own self-awareness in terms of how we each show up in our lives. A successful manager exercises this agency and lives by this hope daily, gently reminding others when they forget.

Reflection Pointers:

- Does sustainable leadership from an inside-out approach work?
- What triggers my inner world and how do I respond?
- Do I like the way I respond or am I reacting to others, situations, and my circumstances?
- How do people respond/react towards me in difficult, stressful situations? What do I do with this feedback?
- Is there a way to improve my thinking process?
- How am I coping with my own workload?
- Do I find it challenging to work with other people?
- Where can I get enough support to help me thrive?
- Why are we not headed in the direction I would like us to go? Am I missing some important details?

VI

CO-PROSPERITY AS A VALUE

Are We Ready To Give And Receive, In Balance?

The Japanese attempted a co-prosperity model after the Second World War; they called it Japan's Co-Prosperity Sphere, according to a journal article published in 1943.[130] This concept was 'an expression of hope for the Japanese people who had no clear idea of the purposes of the war' and extended to occupied territories with a proposal for India's inclusion for the economic bloc to 'be self-sufficient and more complete and powerful than any of the other economic blocs which were to be formed after the restoration of peace'.[131]

Fast-forward to more recent times, in their book *Demanding Sustainability: Pillars to (Re-)Build a Shared Prosperity*, Morrissey and Heidkamp outline five pillars in sharing prosperity since the aftermath of the COVID-19 global shock. The five pillars are ecological prosperity, a decarbonised economy, a shared (cost) burden, a transformative social sustainability, and a just

---

130 A.J. Grajdanzev, 'Japan's Co-Prosperity Sphere', *Pacific Affairs*, 16(3), 311–328, Sep 1943, https://doi.org/10.2307/2751531.

131 Grajdanzev, 'Japan's Co-Prosperity Sphere'; Japanese Empire, Manchuria, China proper, the Philippines, the Netherland Indies, French Indo-China, Thailand, British Malaya, Burma, and to some extent, the Soviet Far East.

resilience.[132] They argue our business-as-usual economy is carbon intensive, fragmented governance, sectoral interest based, and resource extractive. In order to leap to a decarbonised and sustainable economy, we need governance and policy responses targeted at (i) sectoral, (ii) institutional, (iii) regional, (iv) community levels in order to build a restorative relationship with the ecosphere and distributive, procedural, and restorative justice for resilience. These principles for accelerated 'bounce forward' recovery, as they call it, will help us achieve just, sustainable and resilient outcomes.[133]

These ideas have been ruminating in our collective consciousness. Different governments, businesses, organisations have their own way of looking at sharing prosperity, and these respective road maps will hopefully one day lead us to more equitable outcomes for all.

However, that reality is still a far-fetched one, given how many of our societies are taking two steps forward and five steps back. Also, for reasons explained in previous chapters, we cannot see all the moving variables within systems. Chaos is inevitable, and how we prepare for crisis and unexpected events to future-proof ourselves, our organisations, and our societies is the only key. This, as discussed, requires grounded action—honest self-reflections, transparent engagement with stakeholders, vulnerability, and co-creating sustainable solutions together. It also requires giving and receiving in balance, within boundaries acceptable for each one of us, defined by our own sense of self-worth—dignity.

This is why this book hopes to illuminate how we may perhaps reach our visions or hopes for a better, more harmonious future, starting with us. From an individual level, as influencers in our private and public spheres, we can scale up. Having co-prosperity as a value can help us strengthen the practice of our own and others' dignity.

We can appreciate that by harnessing its seven benefits as shown in figure 28; we can pour back into the very thing we are building next so that people, planet, and profits can reach higher heights. And we must try to

i)   Gather complete information from understanding the bigger picture of how our systems run;

---

[132]   J. Morrissey and C.P. Heidkamp, *Demanding Sustainability: Pillars to (Re-)Build a Shared Prosperity*, New Haven, Palgrave Macmillan, 2022, p.180, **[e-book]**.

[133]   Morrissey and Heidkamp, *Demanding Sustainability*, pp. 163-166.

ii) Appreciate wisdom from free-flowing information sharing evident within trustworthy communities;

iii) Practise gratitude for the feedback-providing mechanisms to tweak and improve as we move forward;

iv) Nurture milestones achieved to build more resilient capabilities and reach newer heights;

v) Illuminate ourselves and systems through shifts in mental models, operational systems, and advancement as individuals and collective groups;

vi) Gain tangible outcomes in the form of change, transformation, and movement especially towards upward growth, though not possibly linear (we reinforce the value of our own worth and that of others as well);

vii) Yield all-encompassing, recurring, and regenerative outcomes.

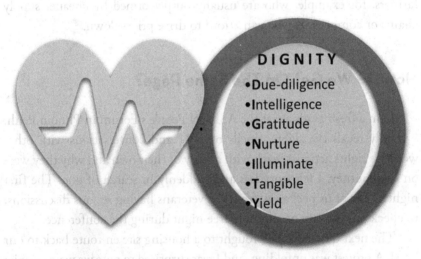

Figure 28: Recap from chapter 1

Practising reciprocity, with its strong correlation with interdependence, will strengthen our co-prosperity muscle. This does not overwrite any existing business norms. We are transforming it from a transactional, quid-pro-quo process to an adjacent possibilities analysis for complementary growth. This means investing some time in the beginning to understand each other's business models and needs, to create synergetic partnerships where together, two entities can do even better than if they were by themselves. Harnessing this power of interdependence will help us achieve the accelerated 'bounce forward' recovery to achieve just, sustainable, and resilient outcomes.

'The most powerful ideas are the ones that set forth an agenda for reform and renewal, the ones that turn a company into a cause.'[134] Jeffrey Hollender in his book *The Responsibility Revolution* shares various examples of such companies, one of which is the cooperative model of business ownership. This model dates back to the mid-nineteenth century to the present with 800 million people involved.[135] It is a mission-oriented business model that is values-driven, with stakeholder-owned companies to sustain a sense of control through consensus-building because with shared values, people reach common ground quicker.[136] Further, as cooperatives are not valuation-driven per se, they can afford to think more long-term and set dignified pricing, forecast supply, and demand trends and offer long-term contracts to help expand each other's business for family-owned farmers, for example, who are usually outperformed by cheaper supply chains or competitors who can afford to drive prices down.[137]

How Do We Get On The Same Page?

I am a fresh graduate at the ASEAN People's Forum in Phnom Penh. I vividly recall the sights, smells of 2011 and conversations with other women's rights activists, each with a story of their own and why they were on this journey. I felt story-less and suddenly in search of one. The first night, a few of us peel away from the veterans having serious discussions, to check out the city on our only free night during the conference.

The next day, we were brought to a housing site en route back to our hotel. A protest was unfolding, and I was surprised to note we were its chief guests. Media reporters were by the side as our Cambodian hosts briefly updated us to show our solidarity as this community was being evicted because of a land development tender approved by the government with

[134] J. Hollender and B. Breen, *The Responsibility Revolution: How the Next Generation of Businesses Will Win,* San Francisco, Jossey-Bass, 2010, p.97, [**e-book**].
[135] Hollender and Breen, *The Responsibility Revolution*, p. 103.
[136] Hollender and Breen, *The Responsibility Revolution*, p. 109.
[137] Hollender and Breen, *The Responsibility Revolution*, pp.91-2.

foreign developers. Unaware, I observed silently as a spokesperson from the evicted community spoke aggressively about the injustices they had faced. I surveyed the site and was surprised to see so much waste piled up right next to their four-storey colony of two buildings. And children were playing close by. My thoughts were disrupted—we had to take a group photo now and were soon enough in the coach. I sat staring out into the horizon and could see more developments being constructed as well.

Development at the expense of people is a story as old as time. Some governments do it right, others not so much. There are constraints involved, either business-political agendas or the need to quickly develop to attract more foreign investment and growth as a result. The means to a plausibly important end where the whole of society progresses with more economic opportunities can still be re-evaluated.

'Are we on the same page?' often comes a tad too late in any discussion because we each come with our own assumptions and goals, unwilling to listen and respond instead. Should one of us be willing, the likelihood of being persuaded or reaching a deadlock escalates, and opportunities for authentic understanding are lost. With lack of time and trust, this escalates faster.

This experience in itself has its purposes to help us uncover our own difficulties in communication, much less for another. Therefore, it will be useful for us to first get on the same page with our own goals—is this a high-value request or one that will seed further discord? Most times, when we are compliant or apathetic, we do not care too much about the nuances, and that is harmful.

The answer to this is often felt in our gut. When something is not right, we just know it. And when we proceed with it because we think we have no other choice for now and/or we are incapable of thinking of better solutions and/or this is what we are allocated in life and so we must stick with it, we suffer. This is what chapter 2, 'Overcome Powerlessness', refers to. We get to a state of powerlessness when these experiences add up, eating at our very sense of self-worth—dignity.

The just transition therefore requires a more empathic approach to understand behavioural psychology, social factors, and resource hurdles in real time. It requires us to exercise agency in self-leadership where we look to strengthening each other's dignity.

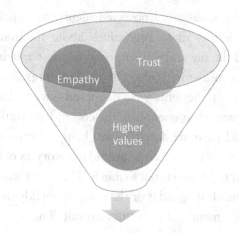

Just transition

Figure 29: A tall order—behaviour change will require
building trust, empathy, and higher values

Behaviour Change Required

Digital advancement has its benefits—faster and better connectivity, especially to remote areas with cheaper telecommunication costs. But it does come with more smoke and mirrors and information overload. As virtual communications overtake face-to-face, given our cross-market operations and/ or hybrid working arrangements, building trust will need to be even higher on the agenda. And this is where more compassionate understanding, especially in providing the benefit of the doubt and space for the other to show up as they are, will be needed. As we know, inherent and unknown lack of trust seeds more confusion, especially where self-leadership and support systems may be weaker. Managing these vulnerabilities with adequate behavioural change will be necessary. Governments and banks, for instance, are already socialising their retail customers to be more mindful of scams and not to make sensitive banking or financial information available to scammers.

But governments and other organisations can only do so much. An awakening to culture and how we organise ourselves and, most importantly, think, behave, and act is upon us. When we unpack this, we disclose the intrinsic motivation and needs of our time. Different generations have their nuances, just as different racial, religious, sexual, interest (and the list goes on) for types of groupings. The ability to first be able to rely on oneself to trust and adapt as crisis emerges will support the social fabric of societies greater, in the long run.

What are we striving for when we say 'just transition'? In Minouche Shafik's book *What We Owe Each Other*, she shares that 'the determinants of subjective well-being are the key elements of the social contract such as good health and meaningful work'. In fact, research on 153 parliamentary elections across Europe since the 1970s show that citizens' subjective satisfaction with their lives is a better predictor of their vote than traditional economic indicators like unemployment and inflation.[138]

As we move through time and various transitions we have made in the name of technological, economic, and social advancement, there are possibilities we can do less of something and more of something else to improve our sense of well-being. This ability should be a policy priority as much as tending to the emergent urgent issues of our times. With this priority, we may have a better chance at regenerative social models where nature and how we exist can coexist. Figure 30 below provides a high-level comparative model of where we have been, where we are at, and where we can be.

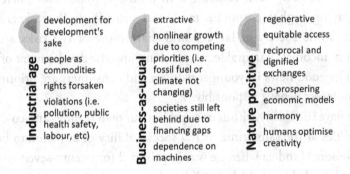

Figure 30: Just transition needs to be a nature-positive one

Shafik proposes a new social contract based off her tenure at the International Monetary Fund (IMF), one that is complementary, not a substitute of governments' willingness to deliver on citizens' expectations,

138 S. Minouche, *What We Owe Each Other: A New Social Contract for a Better Society*, New Jersey, Princeton University Press, 2021, Chapter 8: Getting there: The politics of a new social contract, p.385 **[e-book]**.

especially in Africa, Latin America, the Middle East, and South Asia.[139] She proposes a fairer international tax system, to avoid $500–600 billion of income from corporate tax being lost annually because of globalised supply chains, where companies can manage their books to legally base themselves in any number of places to reduce their tax burden.[140] This affects developing countries the most. She proposes hikes in carbon taxes 'to a level that reduces the risks of catastrophic climate change'. An estimated $49 per tonne increase can make the poorest 10 per cent of the US population better off.[141]

In Shafik's opinion, 'a new social contract with business should focus instead on creating more winners by investing in education and skills, by bringing better infrastructure to deprived areas and by promoting innovation and productivity, all of which reduce the need for redistribution or compensation'.[142] We need to change what is expected of the private sector, and her caveat is that this need not be an increase in overall tax burdens on business. 'Instead, it may be possible to raise corporate tax rates but also reduce payroll taxes by funding core unemployment benefits, minimum pensions, some training costs, and parental leave from general taxation'.[143] A new social contract with business would have (therefore) firms paying higher corporate taxes and providing all workers with benefits, while society at large would share more of the risks around minimum incomes, parental leave, pensions, and the development of new skills. The good news is, younger workers and consumers are prioritising how employers behave responsibly.[144]

We have the ability within us to project our own realities and co-create our realities at the same time. It is a special ability of any human being. Take Nelson Mandela when he was imprisoned for twenty-seven years at Robben Island. He could have chosen hate, revenge; instead, he picked reconciliation and forgiveness. So can we.

---

[139] S. Minouche, *What We Owe Each Other: A New Social Contract for a Better Society*, New Jersey, Princeton University Press, 2021, p.385 **[e-book]**.

[140] Minouche, *What We Owe Each Other*, pp. 233-36.

[141] Minouche, *What We Owe Each Other*, pp. 379-383.

[142] Minouche, *What We Owe Each Other*, pp. 372.

[143] Minouche, *What We Owe Each Other*, pp.373-4.

[144] Minouche, *What We Owe Each Other*, Chapter 7: Generations.

Four Steps To Co-Prosperity

There is no doubt that the only thing that matters to all of us is happiness. We all want to be happy, and we seek this through many different ways, some healthy, some not, especially when not in moderation. How then may we reconcile this and reach authentic happiness?

Buddha replies succinctly: 'Ignorance is from suffering'. This just means we all need to get more aware about ourselves and what is actually happening around us. Most times we are only seeing one part of the whole picture; sometimes we know this and still we let ourselves fall into our habitual thinking and react based on previous experiences. Neuroplasticity can help us undo this, but first it comes with awareness.

This requires willpower to gain awareness—willpower to start recognising our own worth and similar worth that is present in everyone else, no matter what. This requires suspension of judgement and holding space for ourselves and others. It requires a daily commitment to do better, to keep up and ensure we are happy. Happiness is not the absence of everything else. It is an empowered state of being that understands that things are chaotic, people are unpredictable and on their own journeys, and we can still stay grounded in knowing our own worth and building the reality we want. Being self-assured that no one else can take this sense of well-being from us is true happiness because challenges will come our way as we are here to learn and grow. It is how we perceive and overcome them that matters most.

Managing these expectations and allowing growth to take place by reframing will be helpful in sustaining happiness. Willpower is hence enabling. With these conscious efforts to reach happiness that is doing no harm to anyone else, our mindsets will have to evolve. It is almost automatic to match the state of wellness we are aiming for. When we do this, the space around shifts as well because we are all relational beings. When we see someone succeeding in what we are aspiring towards (remember we all want to be happy), after gaining sufficient willpower to build our inner reserves and sense of worth, we too will be influenced. This leads to successful behavioural change, one that is organic and from within for the highest good for all.

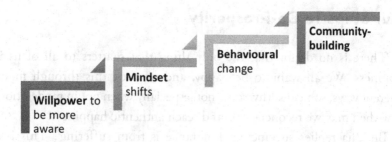

Figure 31: Authentic happiness starts with the uncomfortable truths about ourselves and our environments, then true shifts begin

Power Of Symbiosis

Co-prosperity will only work when we truly want to help ourselves and others succeed. This is premised on a healthy definition of give and take, within the boundaries of everyone involved. Each one of us can embody this value through our different roles and vocations. There is no special career path or requirement to co-prosper.

Given sustainability is a complex and multi-stakeholder action gap, there is certainly scope to implement co-prosperity here. Money, capital infusion, returns on investment will remain important for some time as our trading markets catch up on including social value into stock exchanges, besides a purist quantitative understanding of value in society. It is growing increasingly clear that money is not the sole denomination that can save us from emerging risks. Carbon credits are becoming one mechanism where carbon avoided in one project can be used to offset excess carbon from another.

Besides this, social value created from new jobs in marginalised communities can be used to, well, offset companies that do not hire fairly, perhaps? Probably not, no company will actively disclose that. We all like to think we are diverse and progressive. But some other form of exchange mechanism might emerge, given we need to balance out many inequities in our global system, from wealth disparities to gender wage gap or economic participation, for that matter, due to caregiver burden or differences in hiring and educational access.

Being aware of our own biases, especially those deep within us, will be necessary, as well as the assumptions we have of people we just met or do not know well. Much of it is inherited or absorbed from our lineages and environments growing up. And we can safely decondition over time, should we have the willpower as mentioned above.

Helping others succeed would then become the next step once we achieve sustainable self-leadership. We are able to see the world as it is, overcome our previous states of powerlessness, and own what we can know about a given situation, knowing that 'knowing is still not enough', in Donella Meadows's words.[145] Now we are able to start prioritising others to succeed in embracing co-prosperity as a value and eventually a reality.

The SDGs have one meta-aim: to leave no one behind. When this is the mission, the focus is clear. We have to help others. This is beyond self-sacrificial 'pack your bags and head to the nearest aid relief zone to provide humanitarian support'. Well-meaning endeavours aside, we need to ensure we are leading ourselves sustainably. This means oxygen masks on ourselves first before putting it on others. Most times, we either forget that because it might be too scary to look into our own health issues or we have been socialised to think we need to keep going and self-care is a luxury. These are common and understandable mental models that we can slowly unlearn.

We find the balance within ourselves by working towards our authentic happiness, which is a state of conscious co-creation with the realities we are dealt so that we are not overwhelmed and incapacitated by it. This might be a different definition from mainstream thinking about happiness where it is all joy, smiles, and laughter. Sure, that is the cherry on top, but the base of authentic happiness is this unshakable sense of well-being that your mind is yours, your body is yours, and your abilities are limitless. Too many of us have been told otherwise, and it is becoming generationally tougher to upend this inner turmoil so many of us face as we pile it on and pass it to the future generations. It has to end at some point, and it is safe now. We can let go.

---

[145]　W. Dyer, *Your Sacred Self: Making the Decision to Be Free*, New York, HarperCollins e-books, 2008, Part III: Transcending Our Ego Identities.

Figure 32: How to leave no one behind

How Do We Measure This Change?

Depending on how fast we want to effect change, we can get started with pilot attempts that are smaller in scale. We may use the table below, covering a holistic range of EGSEE indicators which can be further customisable based on organisational vision and mission for sustainability. The logic of the table is to uncover where we might be able to optimise our resources better and if we created new value after all. As I have worked in both nonprofit and corporate sectors, value creation does not require big money or manpower. Often, willpower and stakeholder buy-in can bring about equally sustained efforts, if not more sustained, to an initiative that can be a win-win for everyone involved. Brokering these intricacies will require insights from newcomers and independent facilitators to help see as we might be too used to governance structures or protocols to see alternative possibilities available for us.

To get to sustainable sustainability, we need to do more and do good to the resources we procure, including what we do with it in its end-of-life process. We can improve our responsible consumption quotient and loop back as many resource bits into the circular economy systems available in our orbits. Understandably, infrastructure for particular waste streams might still be in the pipeline, and perhaps we could find other solutions.

There is a need for more mobilised action from the ground up to help complement and supplement the macro policies and initiatives by our governments. Also, it is just good business, good branding to be sustainable. Meetings without plastic bottles or single-use paper cups—win! More healthy food options as opposed to a big buffet spread—win! The table below provides a bit more thinking around this logic flow to closing our resource gap, following by the next logic diagram on how we are closing the loop on resources we use to try to be as circular as possible.

Indicators	Resources used	Value created	Resources wasted
Time	*List line items, activities	xx% time saved solving system errors	*Compare between planning and implementation stage
Financial balance sheet		xx% new investments in ESG projects/funding	
Manpower allocation		xx% increase in manpower productivity due to relevant trainings and complementary use of tech solutions (i.e. generative AI, etc.)	
Compliance related activities (i.e. standards update training, audits, industry consultations, etc)		xx% increase in trust indicators under stakeholder materiality assessment / audits cleared with zero non-conformances (NC)	
Communi cations focus (i.e. from corporate affairs to branding, marketing)		xx% of communications helped consumers understand how to use eco-friendly offerings better	
Procurement process and invoices		xx% of suppliers compliant with procurement policy; xx% of suppliers are ESG certified	

Stakeholder feedback (i.e. customer satisfaction)		xx% stakeholders trust in company offering/ brand, will stay loyal
Health/ wellness promotion		xx MC days avoided by xx employees; absentee rate decreased by xx%
Safety of workers		xx% reduction in safety incidents, xx% compliance observed in risk assessments/ internal audits

Table 5: Leadership review and gaps analysis checklist

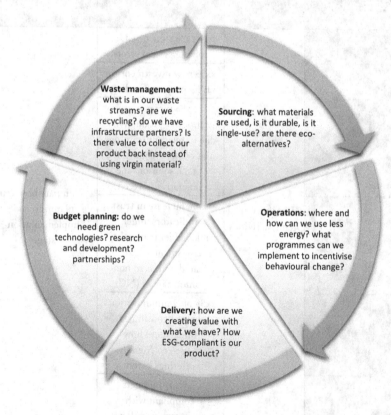

Figure 33: Closing the circular economy loop

We have reached the end of this book. My hope is that there is something hopeful in these pages, new thoughts or ideas came to you, and most importantly, you may have found a strategy or two useful for your own personal and professional growth. The value of co-prosperity and dignity of all are not new concepts, and as ancient knowledge always does, it saves us from recreating new ways of being and functioning. We have all the answers within us to succeed. It is a matter of finding our way home to unlock these gems.

Reflection Pointers:

- Who are we benchmarking to?
- Are we aware of how well we are using our resources and opportunities to optimise them further?
- What are the exact social outcomes we are pursuing and how are we going to achieve it in the most straightforward way?
- Where are we right now with our organisational responsibilities? Are we able to do more or do we need time?
- How is quality measured in our organisations and who does this satisfy the most? Does it bring us intangible value we may have missed?
- Who can we work with to build our own model of co-prosperity?
- How does my organisation define co-prosperity?
- Are there areas where my business or organisation can make simple changes to contribute more to society or stakeholders we work with?
- Where are we at right now with our co-prosperity status and where would we like to be in the near term (i.e. 2030)?

▲

EPILOGUE

Quantum Leap To Transformative Leadership

ugaad is an Indian approach to problem-solving, or rather, an attitude that no matter the challenge, the solution can be found often in the most obvious places or most unorthodox of conceptions with just what you have. We witnessed it everywhere from the taxis with overhung luggage tied cleverly with just one string to bumping a few people off their flight to onboard forty foreigners and detour the flight plan to land us first, while announcing it mid-air to the rest of the passengers. Wait, what?

The announcement just made that the flight would land in Amritsar first before Delhi had some rumblings of discontent. I apologised to my fellow passenger who shared with me that this was the first time he was experiencing such an inconvenience as he commuted back home weekly. But he did not mind it so much since he had read about us in the news and knew this was an important trip for the group of us as we were on invitation from the Indian government.

I sat back, surprised because this mutual understanding would be amiss in other more 'democratic, procedural' places—wait, India is one of the biggest democracies in the world. Then what is it in their system that allows such flexibility to problem-solve with variances of accommodation? While some passengers were bumped off this flight for us, our original flight was cancelled with no rescheduling plan or forewarning. While we waited for hours with no updates and meetings cancelled on the other end of our destination, the jugaad materialised as such.

In this regard, my life has felt like many jugaad strung together to make this book come through. As a final-year undergraduate with literally 'the whole world is your oyster' mindset, I set off to pursue what was both uncommon and paths uncharted when I received an email on the Master's of Human Rights and Democratisation course (Asia Pacific) with opportunities to study both in Sydney and Asia. It was one of those spotlight moments, you know. You are in your tutorial class and the monotony of the proceedings is happening and the laptop notification comes through. Spotlight's on you, you feel illuminated, and it feels like the sign you have been waiting for. So I proceed, right, applied for it despite its exorbitantly high tuition fees, which I was not sure how I was going to pay. So jugaad numero uno came to be. I noticed they had a scholarship since the degree is also for working professionals. I deferred my acceptance and sought out *the* human rights expert in Singapore, and everything else just fell into place.

I did work with one of the toughest and most passionate bosses of bosses. And it appears this trait continued with the rest of my bosses I chose to work with—all have a daring conviction to be the best in their industry with equally strong personality and presence, to boot. I wanted to be in their auras, learn all about how they got there and became the golden girls of their industry.

It was not easy, has not been, and now I know why. The path uncharted rarely is, but the views are amazing. In my first role, I got to travel the region quite a bit, mainly for capacity-building workshops and lobbying meetings in the realms of child rights, women's rights, and social protection floor. Understanding the state of women and children in Asia was eye-opening, and to meet the many civil society representatives, including Association of Southeast Asian Nations (ASEAN) representatives building common ground to advance policies and national legislations to recognise dignity of all, was inspiring. Through my time with the International Council on Social Welfare, I got to work with social agency government directors and executive directors of various non-governmental organisations advocating for their stakeholder groups varying from the elderly to women to citizens.

Understanding how a social protection floor is different from safety nets was equally stimulating. Essentially, a net has holes, right? With a safety net, which was first used to capture the essence of capturing people as they fall (like off a building), there are still gaps to fall through especially if too big. With a floor, imagine the floor you are standing on: it is concrete, and while an earthquake like COVID-19 can break it apart, it is largely still solid foundation. This is what is being advocated as basis for us all to achieve dignity for all. To ensure governments are able to provide that level of social security to support citizens in meeting their basic needs and to in turn contribute back to the economy. This unfortunately is challenging, given the many socio-economic intricacies and even cultural understanding when it comes to social protection.

I was prepared for my master's with all these relevant and tangible experiences. But I was flying into Sydney slightly jaded, burnt-out, and looking for hope instead, a sharp contrast to my bright-eyed undergraduate version. Human rights is a 24/7 battle to keep up with, and I was not sure if this space was sustainable. On the meaningful level, it hits the jackpot, but I had to find out how others coped with its daily stressors, especially when violations and injustices prevail in different corners of our world and still affect us somehow. Australians know this best, with the refugee crisis, for instance. My time in Sydney zoomed by from the sheer amount of coursework we had while living and learning more about the country and its policies. One day, we venture further into Chinatown and bump into a local representative. She is a stunning Caucasian with a hijab, and we talk. We tell her we are students of human rights and we have come from different countries and we are closing up our semester with a week intensive on refugee studies. And she talks about how she knows someone who provides legal counsel pro bono at the Villawood detention centre. I am immediately all ears, and we are at Villawood the following weekend, not knowing what to expect. Frankly, I did not think twice. This was one of the most talked-about topics during our time in Australia, and we just had to be at the scene.

When my professor found out, she was appalled and also amazed how we got there. She then quickly dived into how we were lucky to not have witnessed anything that could have affected us mentally, emotionally and not to do this again. Unknown to us, the detention centre is not someplace one enters to just volunteer their time, given many of its inhabitants are escaping war-torn, conflict-driven, and poverty-stricken conditions. We only understood this further in our intensive week when we interviewed a panel of refugees who now call Australia home. One man in particular remains etched in my mind. When asked if he could go back, would he, he replied with this deep longing for home that you can only recognise if you were torn from what you deeply love and treasure. 'Yes, that was my home.' He was a political refugee.

Safety and all notions of it came to the fore many times through my life experiences—what it means to an average person, how we take it for granted when we have it, and what we do when we do not have it. I read the extent of how many risk their lives to cross over to Europe or Australia with little in hand, families left behind, all in the hope of a better tomorrow. Many do not succeed, some drown, some die from ill health or accidents, others who do survive are no longer themselves. Post-traumatic stress gets swept under the rug of survival in a new country, new language, new people. There is no jugaad for this, unfortunately, except accepting these challenging truths.

We are well onto our second semester in Nepal—Never-Ending Peace and Love, clearly coined by a hippie tourist who got high on Fishtail, which is not an easy track, by the way, but the views—amazing. Anyway, it's the dead cold of winter, and this was my year of winter, with Sydney in the southern hemisphere and Nepal in the northern. I was prepared-ish. No, not really. We were going to really see how things run in Kathmandu from load-shedding to public transportation to feudalism. Yes, unfortunately despite the end of the constitutional monarchy, the societal structures are still hard to overcome and, with it, its privileges and stigmas unless you make it out, meet a foreigner, get enlightened. Here the jugaad for us was how we were going to survive for the next semester. Our college was located two districts away from Kathmandu, and we were used to certain conveniences and had to be in the city centre to have that access. Also, it had to be safe. We had to pay a premium for this, by living right smack in the diplomatic core, in case earthquake or conflicts broke out. The bed did shake, I did move left-right-left, and I was up. That morning alarm was a small quake somewhere, although not to the scale of the destruction that occurred soon after we left in 2015.

We left Sydney, worn out. One of our last panels was with professionals from various international aid and humanitarian organisations, and burnout was very real in this line of work. They did not have much to reply on coping with it. Now in Kathmandu, the pace was much slower, problems with the systems quite visible and mired politics, Never-Ending Peace and Love had to be the answer. From the Boudhanath Stupa to Manakamana Temple, we travelled, we observed, we learnt to slow down. There was one clear-sky day where we could enjoy the Everest mountain range in the horizon with its snow-capped mountains. That was enough.

With this newfound attitude, I returned busy Singapore with this inner knowing that human rights was not the space that generates sustainable energy. It is stuck in precepts and mental models of lack and rigidity. Even advocates had a victim mindset to some extent and blaming the other was easier than taking responsibility, which gets complicated in a time-space continuum with overloaded systems, so many moving variables and lack of clarity on what exactly is happening.

I then figured, despite these experiences, I became a really good researcher. Let us try a think tank next. And the four years that ensued after was stimulating, meaningful again until it plateaued. Track 2, diplomacy, as it is known, has its opportunities to make normative changes as much as policy depending on the right time, right place, right people. Understanding this nuance is what differentiates a good diplomat from a diplomat. Continuing my streak with amazingly talented and committed bosses, my German directors were no different. I travelled the region again, expanding to South Asia and East Asia with yearly autumn meetings in Berlin or Brussels. We had meetings and audiences with international and national leaders. On the outside, this was very exciting-looking, but I was searching for that inner sense of meaning-making. What were all these efforts amounting to? And this took a dip for me when I experienced a few of our stakeholder country politics decline in their democratic consolidation process. And in the words of my first German director as we were walking on the cobbled streets of Erfurt to our meeting, 'Dillpreit, you must know, we are in this boat that is already sinking, and what we are doing is taking the water out to try to stay afloat. You must know this.' If I could include a mind-blown emoji here, I would. Agreed. There has to be a way though, no?

This began the next part of my journey—there has to be a way. I am now in one of the four I* organisations, or was it I-star organisations? Basically, the key nonprofits driving community building for Internet policy and governance. I am unaware where I have landed because this becomes a short but very insightful experience. This time, I am working for a young, ambitious, and former diplomat of a boss. He is equally ambitious with me, and I am attending meetings in Vanuatu and the following week in Kuala Lumpur and then Seoul and then Barcelona, and you get the picture. Each of these meetings equally intense: How do we strengthen a fragmenting Internet? How do we limit bad actors? How do we get more community members to join a technical space? What are the opportunities for younger students to participate? Are everyone's rights well represented in this space? How do we govern the Internet with a multi-stakeholder model and reach consensus?

I had no jugaad for this experience. I just lived it from one meeting to another and reached a crescendo at the Nepal Internet Governance Forum. Thankfully, load-shedding is no longer a bane since my postgraduate days.

Multi-stakeholder governance is a real level playing field. Coming from international relations, where governments rule as the main decision-makers, here in the Internet world, everyone is on the same plane of existence with equal say, although personally I think the techies dominate this world. If you have studied the domain name system or Internet protocol types, you will know why. It is an elite space in my opinion, with so many outside of this loop, which definitely scared me. I tried my best to let many people know about this, but maybe it works out that most of us are also not that interested in how things are really run in our world as long as it works!

We are still in silos; we are still seen as separate, different from each other. And as for the technology, I am glad quantum computing is coming up. With children learning to code and attempting man-in-the-middle attacks, and bad actors always more advanced with their dark web, the vulnerabilities of our information systems need a reboot if not overhaul, which will come in due time once we move into a time and space designed to be less defensive and open instead. At some point, '.onion' needs to be considered the Internet and this world as well.

Now I am at a crossroads, do I keep moving through this mist? What am I really searching for? What am I going to find?

The year 2019 began with a vipassana retreat in Chiang Mai, which was uncomfortable. Unaware that I was awakening to the truth of myself,

I had to first learn to sit still and by myself. This was another difficult experience since I had been a people person for most of my life, and I believed I had no bandwidth to just sit still. In January of 2019, everything just came to a standstill for me. Imagine you are shooting a movie and then someone just shuts off the power source and the whole set and crew leave, and you are wondering what happened and why it is so dark all of a sudden. With a vague idea of starting a business of my own, I ventured overseas in search for the elixir of success. Something would come through.

I take a break from this in 2020, right before the gradual lockdowns of the world. This time, I am working with traditional media, academics, mobile journalists, and mobile-gear businesses to convene a regional network to share knowledge and build business acumen in an increasingly digital and smartphone world where news needs to be real-time, consumable, and on the mobile, meeting readers where they are at most times. Challenges in this space primarily circled around misinformation and disinformation. With so much information, available at a click, we need to be better at discerning facts from fake news and deepfakes as well.

Harvard Kennedy School surveyed 150 academic experts to identify expert consensus and views still differed.[146] While it is agreed that misinformation refers to false and misleading information, how important the intent behind spreading fake news and what is defined as misinformation was divided. Lack of knowledge was not a key reason for this happening. People who believe and share fake news do so from motivated reasoning, political partisanship, inattention, lack of cognitive reflection, or repeated exposure. Social media platforms have exacerbated this situation. Appropriate platform design changes, algorithmic changes, content moderation, deplatforming prominent actors that spread misinformation, and crowdsourcing misinformation detection or removal

[146] S. Altay, M. Berriche, H. Heuer, J. Farkas and S. Rathje, 'A survey of expert views on misinformation: Definitions, determinants, solutions and future of the field', Harvard Kennedy School, 27 July 2023, https://misinforeview.hks.harvard.edu/article/a-survey-of-expert-views-on-misinformation-definitions-determinants-solutions-and-future-of-the-field/ (accessed 26 January 2024).

could help manage the situation, factoring in what people think and respect for individuals' right to information.[147]

If the global pandemic has taught us anything, it's that accurate and clear information is life-saving. How many of us fell prey to disinformation regarding remedies to avoid contracting the virus or that some of us were naturally immune to a rapidly growing virus? And if we did not know better, because the person telling us this may be a respected individual who strayed for a second, we believe it and pass it on or internalise it to be more fearful of someone or something.

For me, completely grounded for the first time in my life, like everyone else, I had to question who I was if I did not travel. And for the first time, I also had to unpack this 'busy' notion so many of us hide behind. On one hand, it was easier since most of us could not go places and have as much access to distractions, except maybe digital TV options booming along with other virtual experiences. Since I had to work on my business plan to assuage worried family and friends that I was not idling, I oscillated between meditating, shadow work, and working on my laptop. Iteration after iteration, I researched and read, realising the system actors in sustainability are far too many, which is good news, and at the same time disparate in their efforts, which is why we have not been able to significantly move the needle despite this multi-decade discourse. Financiers had to come on board, but what is this ecosystem and who is in it? How does money flow through investment decisions and market fluctuations?

147 R. Hertwig, S.M. Herzog and A. Kozyreva, 'Blinding to Circumvent Human Biases: Deliberate Ignorance in Humans, Institutions, and Machines'. *Perspectives on Psychological Science*, 0(0), 5 September 2023, https://doi.org/10.1177/17456916231188052.

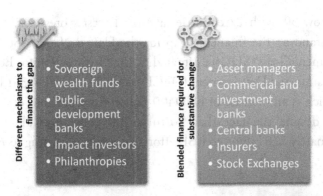

Figure 34: Key financial actors currently engaged or can be engaged to close the sustainable development financing gap

At the height of the global pandemic in the second half of 2020, I started mind-mapping both traditional and alternative financing actors across the world and following the money, so to speak. If the problem in sustainable development is not meeting the goals because of lack of financing, then what can we do about it? A rabbit hole opened, and I fell like Alice. Something must give here; there must be a solution. Why is it so difficult to shift money from oversaturated capital markets or pockets to the hands of those who literally need to survive, those at the bottom of the pyramid, when research shows so much promise but little traction?

At this juncture, I am clearly underestimating the survival instincts of the Slumdog millionaires and many others leveraging peer-to-peer lending, bartering, cooperatives to survive when government systems fail them. However, continuous rapid urbanisation, abrupt demonetisation, and entrenched societal prejudice challenge one's chances for social mobility—an inner violence will naturally brew. I felt it in the movies I watched, the odds stacked against bright minds cordoned off from the accessible lanes to success. This is a story as old as time, I mentally exclaimed, with potato-chip-flavoured fingers as I sank further in finding a solution within the maze, like a mad scientist.

According to Transparency International's Corruption Perceptions Index, global average remains unchanged in a decade at 43 out of 100 points, 100 being very clean and 0 being highly corrupt: 131 countries did not progress against corruption for the tenth year and majority two-thirds score below 50, with 27 countries at their lowest scores ever.[148] This is notwithstanding the financing gap for the United Nations Sustainable Development Goals (SDGs) estimated by the Organisation for Economic Co-operation and Development (OECD) could reach USD4.3 trillion per year, which is an increase of USD400 billion from previous estimates.[149] This is despite the fact that Fortune 500 companies alone devote approximately $20 billion to CSR efforts annually, according to *Forbes*.[150]

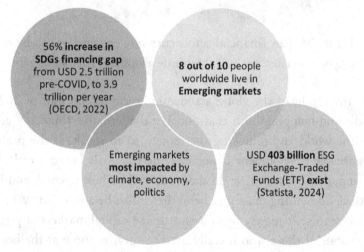

Figure 35: Sustainability financing gap in emerging markets[151]

---

[148] Transparency International, *Corruption Perceptions Index*, 2024, https://www.transparency.org/en/cpi/2022 (accessed 26 January 2024).

[149] OECD, *Bottlenecks to Access Sustainable Development Goals Finance for Developing Countries*, 2023, http://www.oecd.org/g20/oecd-g20-bottlenecks-sdg-finance-developing-countries.pdf (accessed 26 January 2024).

[150] O. Iglesias, *The End of CSR (As We Know It) and the Rise of Businesses with a Conscience*, Forbes, 1 Dec 2022, https://www.forbes.com/sites/esade/2022/12/01/the-end-of-csr-as-we-know-it-and-the-rise-of-businesses-with-a-conscience/?sh=502f12b27f16 (accessed 26 January 2024).

[151] OECD, *Global Outlook on Financing for Sustainable Development 2023: No Sustainability Without Equity*, 10 November 2022, https://www.oecd.org/publications/global-outlook-on-financing-for-sustainable-development-2023-fcbe6ce9-en.htm (accessed 26 January 2024); *ESG investing - statistics & facts*, Statista, 2024. https://www.statista.com/topics/7463/esg-and-impact-investing/ (accessed 26 January 2024).

I had to find out why, and what exactly was going on. And that quickly flipped to 'let me find a solution' instead. Let me take on this mystical mammoth and conjure a unified digital-platform business matching micro enterprises in last-mile markets who need financing with those who can invest/part with funds (philanthropy) or offer risk guarantees for other investors fearful of forex/political instability.

Through this crowdsourced data management platform, let us engage everyone and incentivise local communities where company operations or value chain exists to report on impact caused by businesses on environment and societal progress. With intricate verification processes to ensure crowdsourced data is legitimate, the more socially endorsed a contributor, the greater their ability to monetise the information they provide through the platform. Similarly, companies and organisations that use this data can pay for these insights through a subscription model.

This multifaceted sustainability reporting platform will be self-driven and an inherent multiplier of non-financial data sets that governments and companies alike can leverage to evaluate our performance from a bottom-up approach. With sophisticated technology, this open-source platform, when shared with technology-development operations providers, mentioned a three- to four-year production time to build as well as investment. Good news for me is that this is possible, albeit it will need patient capital and time, which I had run out of for now. Also, news of an international sustainability standards board was announced during this time, with the mandate to converge and present one financial reporting framework that includes material non-financial data as well.

I had to wait to see what would come through. I also had to do something, so I ventured into the world of corporate ESG reporting. Curious to learn of the underlying methodologies behind the likes of Sustainalytics, CDP, GRESB because this big data platform would have its own proprietary algorithms, I studied the scoring frameworks studiously and noted, like many others, that each ESG rating/ranking entity had their own focus and approach. But I soon observed that focusing on data alone is myopic.

Data unfortunately can only reveal so much, and it needs to be clear of human error, which will require several layers of quality check. Many promising software companies offer the ease of data management and analysis, but they still require the bridge to human engagement with the platform even if they might provide the initial data-mapping requirements and uploads with CSV sheets and/or documentation like invoices. Humans are still the most important piece of this digitalisation transition.

Am I against technology now? No, remember the mystical-mammoth solution above—I am still holding out to actualise it maybe when quantum computing is more mainstream. Maybe increasing American and Chinese investment can make it happen quicker.[152] It is just we need to be more intentional as with all other matters of life. What problem exactly are we tackling, and purpose? Is it just for the sake of reporting or are we committed to organisational changes from a longer-term perspective to mitigate and adapt to emerging risks?

At this stage, it looks like convergence of intent to operate with a conscience and profit at the same time will crystallise. It is still a long shot since sustainability has been around for some time; corporate social responsibility was coined as early as the 1950s.[153] With annual UN climate change conferences stepping up year on year (or being stepped up) to address the urgent need to respond and halve greenhouse gas (GHG) emissions, there is hope for humanity. Introducing climate litigation training for judiciary shows promise as well.

It is the end of 2023, and I am leaving a comfortable corporate job. The road ahead is unknown again, and it scares me as much as excites. This book is how I choose to get started, by putting everything I have learnt into actionable insights for sustainable self-leadership. We are all here to be ourselves, provide unique insights, and evolve. My experiences should not be any indication of yours. We are all on unique paths. Hopefully we can all take inspired action back to our wholeness.

---

[152] N.S. Chanda, *Quantum computing: Can China overtake the US?*, *Asia Fund Managers*, 22 August 2023, https://asiafundmanagers.com/sg/quantum-computing-can-china-overtake-the-us/ (accessed 26 January 2024).

[153] A. B. Carroll, Chapter 2: A History of Corporate Social Responsibility: Concepts and Practices', in Andrew Crane, and others (eds.), *The Oxford Handbook of Corporate Social Responsibility*, online edition, Oxford Academic, 2008, https://doi.org/10.1093/oxfordhb/9780199211593.003.0002.

I am grateful for my personal sense-making journey through shadow work, dealing with the disruptions and changes of our times. The perseverance of the human spirit is prevalent as we pivot communication tools, innovating more green technologies and improving accessibility for all through empathy and design thinking so that we can all connect and be heard and seen.

The time to bridge the action gap has come, and we can do this together, honestly (pun intended). We can build organisations through a co-prosperity model and engage everyone to do their part. Even the greenest of buildings would be pointless if maintenance is compromised with unhealthy retrofits to undo the design and intent for hybrid cooling, for instance. Divestment, while strategic at first, would just make it someone else's problem, and to understand this, we need co-prosperity as value and longer-term thinking, which is understandably difficult if shareholders and stakeholders are not on the same page.

With our current business models and ways of operating, it is highly challenging to pivot unless we are forced to, have extra reserves, or comply with a regulatory or international standard. Most of us are guzzling electricity, not monitoring our stakeholders on their resource management plans and wondering how to make reductions. For most of it, this is not a priority yet and business as usual is desired as many organisations think they cannot cope with more changes.

Self-reliance is the ability to stay grounded, to know when to act and how to interpret the information that comes to us. It is about being reliable to ourselves and showing we will not jeopardise our well-being with more fear. Likewise for businesses, self-reliance is about accepting change is a constant. Solutions are available for all issues, and we achieve more results when we work together with others, be it within our companies or between business partners.

Yet this is far from reality. I attended a workshop on *The Art of War* by Sun Tzu once and greatly appreciated that my trainer was ambivalent about the applicability of the teachings today, given it is from a different time where trickery and deception was needed to avert systemic wars, famine, and disruption. Today, no matter how competitive a business landscape is, we need to succeed with others. Business coalitions and partnerships built with best intentions for society can help us mitigate and strategise ways forward that combine our resource pool and information to navigate better and more effectively against the headwinds of change.

Building coalitions to stall this momentum with more discourse is not helpful in the mid to long term. Quickly translating insights to actionable steps will be more crucial by asking, 'What do we do next now that we know what we know?' Win-win solutions based on a transactional rather than a values-based approach keep us in a vicious cycle of business as usual. With a values-based approach such as co-prosperity, we accept change is inevitable, and we can scale new heights together, to bring on a new virtuous cycle—one that is self-sustaining, regenerative, and innovative.

To put it simply and for visualisation purposes, when we try to force a square wooden peg into a round hole and it will not go through even when we stack up other like-minded partners on top of it to create more impact, we need to review. The energy is stuck at most, and breakthrough, which needs to come through with every effort we make, is missing. And because we are all busy being stacked up against each other, we lack space to discuss this. Moving out of this systemic hold and creating space for the new will be helpful.

In relation to leadership credibility, focusing on self-reliance ensures leaders are committed to the business surviving for the long haul and not for short-term gains. It shows that leaders are forecasting and adjusting business strategy accordingly to keep creating value for all stakeholders. Through these actions and mindset, reinvesting earnings is likely as leaders focus on growing business successes.

We will need sustainable leaders, those who do not identify with ego, vanity, or status. Getting to self-reliance is a journey since it is easier to give our power away, especially if there is groupthink. But independence of thought is necessary. Discerning and making decisions that support us and others is even more necessary today than ever, if this book has not made that clear enough already.

However, even though information and data are readily available to us, we may still not know how to make sense of it. For companies, outsourcing it to AI or using generative AI systems to co-create may seem logical, but this may not be sufficient. A new world where each one of us is more self-reliant requires us to understand and know what information we have and need to get where we need to. I am referring to the skill of knowing when there is misinformation or disinformation being presented to us and following an ethical code of conduct that supports accurate discernment.

There are many wisdom thinkers, philosophers, and experienced adventurers who share this need to really deep-dive within ourselves to notice our inherent abilities to break out of any adversity and reach new personal heights if we let ourselves be. To Morgan Freeman, 'courage is key to life itself. A lot of people are born in situations that they say they will never get out of this . . . (or) get out of here . . .' He pauses and continues, 'Man, the bus runs every day.'[154] So why are we in our own way? And if we are already on our way, how are we helping others get there too as sustainable leaders?

> Don't aim at success. The more you aim at it and make it a target, the more you are going to miss it. For success, like happiness, cannot be pursued; it must ensue, and it only does so as the unintended side effect of one's personal dedication to a cause greater than oneself or as the by-product of one's surrender to a person other than oneself. Happiness must happen, and the same holds for success: you have to let it happen by not caring about it. I want you to listen to what your conscience commands you to do and go on to carry it out to the best of your knowledge. Then you will live to see that in the long run—in the long run, I say!—success will follow you precisely because you had forgotten to think about it.
>
> —Austrian Holocaust survivor and psychologist
> Viktor E. Frankl, *Man's Search for Meaning*

---

[154] M. Freeman *Courage is the key to life itself,* CNN, 4 Jun 2014, https://www. youtube.com/watch?v=r72a19Lbz7k (accessed 26 January 2024).

REFERENCE LIST

Al-Mashat, R., *Climate financing that puts people first,* International Monetary Fund: Finance and Development, September 2023, https://www.imf.org/en/Publications/fandd/issues/2023/09/POV-climate-financing-that-puts-people-first-rania-al-mashat (accessed 26 January 2024).

Altay, S., Berriche, M., Heuer, H., Farkas, J. and Rathje, S., *'A survey of expert views on misinformation: Definitions, determinants, solutions and future of the field'*, Harvard Kennedy School, 27 July 2023, https://misinforeview.hks.harvard.edu/article/a-survey-of-expert-views-on-misinformation-definitions-determinants-solutions-and-future-of-the-field/ (accessed 26 January 2024).

Baldo, D. and Baldarelli, M.G., *'Renewing and improving the business model toward sustainability in theory and practice'*, Int J Corporate Soc Responsibility 2, 3, 2017, https://doi.org/10.1186/s40991-017-0014-z

Basel Institute on Governance, *Green Corruption*, 2024, https://baselgovernance.org/green-corruption (accessed 26 January 2024).

Boston Consulting Group, How Insurers Can Innovate in Response to Extreme Weather Events, 10 October 2023, https://www.bcg.com/publications/2023/how-insurers-can-innovate-in-response-to-extreme-weather-events (accessed 26 January 2024).

Briskin, A., Erickson, S., Callanan, T. and Ott, J., *The Power of Collective Wisdom: And the Trap of Collective Folly*, San Francisco, Berrett-Koehler Publishers, 2009.

Cabrejo le Roux, A., *Is the Climate Crisis a Corruption Crisis? An Interview with Brice Bohmer,* Basel Institute on Governance, 30 August 2023, https://baselgovernance.org/news/climate-crisis-corruption-crisis-interview-brice-bohmer (accessed 26 January 2024).

Carroll, A. B., Chapter 2: A History of Corporate Social Responsibility: Concepts and Practices', in Andrew Crane, and others (eds.), *The Oxford Handbook of Corporate Social Responsibility*, online edition, Oxford Academic, 2008, https://doi.org/10.1093/oxfordhb/9780199211593.003.0002

Chanda, N.S., *Quantum computing: Can China overtake the US?, Asia Fund Managers,* 22 August 2023, https://asiafundmanagers.com/sg/quantum-computing-can-china-overtake-the-us/ (accessed 26 January 2024).

Civil Aviation Authority of Singapore (CAAS), *Singapore Is Operationally Ready for Sustainable Aviation Fuel But More Is Needed to Support Adoption*, https://www.caas.gov.sg/who-we-are/newsroom/Detail/singapore-is-operationally-ready-for-sustainable-aviation-fuel-but-more-is-needed-to-support-adoption (accessed 26 January 2024).

Clements, B., Gupta, S., Liu, J., 'Settling the Climate Debt', *Finance and Development*, https://www.imf.org/en/Publications/fandd/issues/2023/09/settling-the-climate-debt-clements-gupta-liu

Copley, M., *Global talks to cut plastic waste stall as industry and environmental groups clash*, NPR, https://www.npr.org/2023/11/20/1214141053/un-plastic-waste-pollution-negotiations-treaty-kenya-fossil-fuel-climate-change (accessed 26 January 2024).

Deloitte, *The Challenge of Double Materiality Sustainability Reporting at a Crossroad*, https://www2.deloitte.com/cn/en/pages/hot-topics/topics/climate-and-sustainability/dcca/thought-leadership/the-challenge-of-double-materiality.html (accessed 26 January 2024).

Dyer, W., *Your Sacred Self: Making the Decision to Be Free*, New York, HarperCollins e-books, 2008.

ESG investing - statistics & facts, Statista, 2024, https://www.statista.com/topics/7463/esg-and-impact-investing/ (accessed 26 January 2024).

Fairhurst, G., *The Power of Framing: Creating the Language of Leadership*, 2nd edition, San Francisco, Jossey-Bass, 2010.

Fogarty, D., *See you in court: training equips Asian judges for climate litigation cases*, The Straits Times, 15 Nov 2023, https://www.straitstimes.com/asia/see-you-in-court-training-equips-asian-judges-for-climate-litigation-cases (accessed 26 January 2024).

Freeman, M., *Courage is the key to life itself*, CNN, 4 Jun 2014, https://www.youtube.com/watch?v=r72a19Lbz7k (accessed 26 January 2024).

Garforth, L., *Green Utopias: Environmental Hope Before and After Nature*, Cambridge, John Wiley and Sons, 2017.

Goleman, D. and P. Senge, P., *Working with Presence: A Leading with Emotional Intelligence Conversation with Peter Senge*, location, Macmillan Audio, unabridged edition, 2006.

Grajdanzev, A.J., 'Japan's Co-Prosperity Sphere', *Pacific Affairs*, 16(3), 311–328, Sep 1943, https://doi.org/10.2307/2751531

Hertwig, R., Herzog, S.M. and Kozyreva, A., 'Blinding to Circumvent Human Biases: Deliberate Ignorance in Humans, Institutions, and Machines'. *Perspectives on Psychological Science*, 0(0), 5 September 2023, https://doi.org/10.1177/17456916231188052

Hicks, D., *Leading with Dignity: How to Create a Culture That Brings Out the Best in People*, New Haven, Yale University Press, 2018.

Hollender, J., and Breen, B., *The Responsibility Revolution: How the Next Generation of Businesses Will Win*, San Francisco, Jossey-Bass, 2010.

Iglesias, O., *The End of CSR (As We Know It) and the Rise of Businesses with a Conscience*, Forbes, 1 Dec 2022, https://www.forbes.com/sites/esade/2022/12/01/the-end-of-csr-as-we-know-it-and-the-rise-of-businesses-with-a-conscience/?sh=502f12b27f16 (accessed 26 January 2024).

Jones, N., *Progress on plastic pollution treaty too slow, scientists say*, Nature, 20 November 2023, https://www.nature.com/articles/d41586-023-03579-1 (accessed 26 January 2024).

Lee, J.H., Aubert, B.A., Barker JR., Risk mapping in community pharmacies. *Journal of Patient Safety and Risk Management*. 2023; 28(2): 59–67. DOI: 10.1177/25160435231154167

Liao, K., *What is the Bridgetown Initiative? What to know about the game-changing plan for climate finance*, Global Citizen, 9 May 2023, https://www.globalcitizen.org/en/content/climate-change-bridgetown-initiative-mia-mottley/ (accessed 26 January 2024).

Long, J., '7 surprising facts to know about the circular economy for COP26', *World Economic Forum*, 2021, 27 October 2021, https://www.weforum.org/agenda/2021/10/7-surprising-facts-to-know-about-the-circular-economy-for-cop26/ (accessed 26 January 2024).

Meadows, D.H., *Thinking in Systems*, Vermont, Chelsea Green Publishing, 2008.

Minouche, S., *What We Owe Each Other: A New Social Contract for a Better Society*, New Jersey, Princeton University Press, 2021.

Morrissey, J. and Heidkamp, C.P., *Demanding Sustainability: Pillars to (Re-)Build a Shared Prosperity*, New Haven, Palgrave Macmillan, 2022.

Nikkei Asia, *Global companies must learn from Thai floods that upended supply chains*, 13 October 2021, https://asia.nikkei.com/Opinion/The-Nikkei-View/Global-companies-must-learn-from-Thai-floods-that-upended-supply-chains (accessed 26 January 2024).

FTSE Russell, *The COP28 Net Zero Atlas*, November 2023, https://www. lseg.com/content/dam/ftse-russell/en_us/documents/research/cop28-net-zero-atlas.pdf (accessed 26 January 2024).

OECD, *Bottlenecks to Access Sustainable Development Goals Finance for Developing Countries*, 2023, http://www.oecd.org/g20/oecd-g20-bottlenecks-sdg-finance-developing-countries.pdf (accessed 26 January 2024).

OECD, *Global Outlook on Financing for Sustainable Development 2023: No Sustainability Without Equity*, 10 November 2022, https://www.oecd.org/publications/global-outlook-on-financing-for-sustainable-development-2023-fcbe6ce9-en.htm (accessed 26 January 2024).

Perreard, S., *Plastic Overshoot Day*, https://plasticovershoot.earth/wp-content/uploads/2023/06/EA_POD_report_2023-V3.pdf, Environmental Action (accessed 26 January 2024).

Rezaee, Z., Tsui, J., Cheng. P, and Zhou, G., *Business Sustainability in Asia: Compliance, Performance, and Integrated Reporting and Assurance*, London, John Wiley and Sons, 2019.

Rhick, L., *No one left behind: Simplified guide hopes to push sustainability disclosures among Malaysian SMEs*, Eco-Business, https://www.eco-business.com/news/no-one-left-behind-simplified-guide-hopes-to-push-sustainability-disclosures-among-malaysian-smes/ (accessed 26 January 2024).

Rosenthal, C. and Jones, N., *Chaos Engineering: System Resiliency in Practice*, California, O'Reilly Media, 2020.

Scharmer, O., 'Turning Toward Our Blind Spot: Seeing the Shadow as a Source for Transformation', *Field of the Future Blog*, Medium, https://medium.com/presencing-institute-blog/turning-toward-our-blind-spot-seeing-the-shadow-as-a-source-for-transformation-aff23d480a55 (accessed 26 January 2024).

Scharmer, O., *Theory U: Leading from the Future as It Emerges*, California, Berrett-Koehler Publishers, 2009.

ScienceDirect Topics, *Chaos Theory - an overview - Discussion 5.6*, 2024, https://www.sciencedirect.com/topics/earth-and-planetary-sciences/chaos-theory (Accessed 5 February 2024).

Sciutto, J., *The Madman Theory: Trump Takes on the World*, New York, Harper, 2020.

Senge, P., *The Fifth Discipline: The Art and Practice of the Learning Organization* (revised and updated version), New York, Doubleday, 2006.

Stewart, I., 'Portraits of chaos: The latest ideas in geometry are combining with high-tech computer graphics – the results are providing stunning new insights into chaotic motion', *New Scientist*, 4 November 1989, https://www.newscientist.com/article/mg12416893-100-portraits-of-chaos-the-latest-ideas-in-geometry-are-combining-with-high-tech-computer-graphics-the-results-are-providing-stunning-new-insights-into-chaotic-motion/ (accessed 29 January 2024).

Straussfogel, D. and Schilling, C. von, Systems Theory. *International Encyclopaedia of Human Geography*, pp. 151–58, 2009, https://www.sciencedirect.com/science/article/abs/pii/B9780080449104007549

Towler, G., *Human Ingenuity Is Key To Climate Action*, Forbes, https://www.forbes.com/sites/honeywell/2023/11/27/human-ingenuity-is-key-to-climate-action/?sh=59f829c19c38 (accessed 26 January 2024).

Transparency International, *Corruption Perceptions Index*, https://www.transparency.org/en/cpi/2022 (accessed 26 January 2024).

UN Department of Economic and Social Affairs, *Policy Brief No. 131: Credit Rating Agencies and Sovereign Debt: Four proposals to support achievement of the SDGs*, United Nations, https://www.un.org/development/desa/dpad/wp-content/uploads/sites/45/publication/PB_131_final.pdf (accessed 26 January 2024).

UN News, *Developing countries face $4 trillion investment gap in SDGs*, 5 July 2023, https://news.un.org/en/story/2023/07/1138352 (accessed 26 January 2024).

Westrum, R., 'A typology of organisational cultures', article, *Quality and Safety in Health Care*, Research Gate Publications, January 2005, https://www.researchgate.net/publication/8150380 (accessed 26 January 2024).

Westrum, R., 'The study of information flow: a personal journey', *Elsevier Safety Science*, August 2014, https://www.researchgate.net/publication/261186680 The study of information flow A personal journey (accessed 26 January 2024).

Ziauddin, S. and Iwona, A., *Introducing Chaos: A Graphic Guide*, London, Icon Books, 2004.

ADDITIONAL RESOURCE

The dignity® Audit,
A Checklist for Healthy Workplaces

The aim of this checklist is to create and nurture healthy workplaces, thriving collaborations and innovative solutions to boost our individual and collective creativity, productivity and outputs. Let's co-prosper together. More information available on www.goalweaver.biz.

dignity® Approach	Reflection Questions for Leadership	Desired state of being
Due diligence	• Are we aware of our workplace attitudes, culture and exchanges - are people working as cohesively as they can or is there friction? • Do we conduct performance appraisals based on team metrics? • How often are these reviews conducted and is it sufficient? • Is the system open to receiving organic feedback from fellow colleagues? • Is there a way to track regular inputs on my team's dynamic and outlook?	✓ I am open to exploring new ways to create a healthy workplace ✓ I believe we work better when we are engaged in what we do ✓ I help others see meaning in what they do ✓ Our deliverables add value to the organisation's development and growth

Intelligence	• What sources make up the collective intelligence of my team? • What are some plausible gaps to help us scale up, get to the next level? • What is the collective pool of contribution from my team? • Who is willing to learn? • Where can I support those struggling? • Are we utilising the core strengths of our talents? • Are we missing someone out? is someone being left behind? • Does my team open up to me / HR? • How are we cultivating trust?	✓ I know what I know ✓ I know who/what/where to learn more ✓ We share relevant information in a timely manner ✓ I respect privacy and create an appropriate culture to inspire my team as well ✓ I receive information that is evidence-based, factual and substantive ✓ We take action when recommended
dignity® Approach	**Reflection Questions for Leadership**	**Desired state of being**
Gratitude	• When was the last time I thanked my team / talents for their contribution? • Have I been grateful of solutions offered to me by my team? • Where have I taken new opportunities or time for self-reflection, for granted?	✓ I am calm and clear headed most times ✓ I accept the complexity of workflows and people management ✓ I am more patient with my team ✓ We work out solutions together / I guide my team towards solutions ✓ I respond instead of reacting ✓ I seek to understand instead of instructing ✓ There are more than one way of getting a task done ✓ I appreciate intergenerational working styles within my team

Nurture	• Am I encouraging the conducive kind of behaviours, attitudes and information sharing that will help everyone get along better and deliver quicker, better or more harmonious exchanges? • Do we create safe spaces for everyone to share their views, to be heard first? • How am I actively listening to what is going around me? • Is being right more important than upholding peace?	✓ I manage issues of 'injustice' by listening to all ✓ I hear different points of view to find common ground ✓ We come to resolutions together, in agreement ✓ We work in a safe space where different ideas and perspectives can be expressed ✓ I understand and help others get over to the other side ✓ I listen to what is really being said
dignity® Approach	Reflection Questions for Leadership	Desired state of being
Illumination	• How can I recognise and contribute to healthy workplace culture? • What will make me see better? widen my outlook on my team and increase my chances of understanding underlying concerns (if any)? • Are we overworked to be looking at this issue? • What is my own bandwidth in managing this situation?	✓ I am open to feedback ✓ I appreciate honesty shared in a calm and professional manner ✓ My team and I have healthy boundaries around work ✓ We manage our time and resources well
Tangible	• How can we create a safe space? • When are we able to listen to one another best? • What are some quick steps my team members and I can take now? • What are some goals that will help us create the right culture? • Where do we want to be in terms of our team cohesion by next quarter/year? • How do I get buy-in?	✓ I identify the need to map our change journey ✓ I accept all small wins along the way ✓ I appreciate the steps we can take towards our goals ✓ We have clear goals defined at the individual and team level ✓ We know when to check in on our progress ✓ We have a clear timeline and targets to meet

dignity® Approach	Reflection Questions for Leadership	Desired state of being
Yield	• What can I expect from adopting dignity? • Has the team shown a difference with their attitude or mindset? • Am I making good on my own goals as a leader? • How have other stakeholders viewed our progress as a team? • Are customers more satisfied? • Have misunderstandings been reduced?	✓ I achieve incremental success together with my team ✓ We are progressing in how we speak, act and show up for each other ✓ I am feeling more balanced than before ✓ We are deciphering appropriate next steps and saving resources ✓ I am/We are satisfied

▲

ABOUT THE AUTHOR

F or the past decade, Dillpreit Kaur has worked with leaders on the cutting edge of sustainability, spanning the private sector, politics, and civil society. With increasing demands to capitalise on these changes, her expertise as a social scientist provides evidence-based insights and solutions with a human-centric approach, encapsulated in this book. Dillpreit has a Master's degree in Human Rights and Democratisation from the University of Sydney and a Bachelors of Social Science (Honours) degree in Political Science from the National University of Singapore.